Erotic New York

PUBLISHED BY HANGOVER MEDIA, INC.
NEW YORK, NEW YORK

Copyright © 2002 Hangover Media, Inc.
Author: Tim Haft

Published by
Hangover Media, Inc.
154 W. 14th St. 9th Floor
New York, NY 10011

Telephone: 212.242.2566
Fax: 212.242.3704
E-mail: info@sheckys.com

CEO: Chris Hoffman
President: Claudia Chan
Senior Editor: Erin McKinnon
Director of Publishing: Pas Niratbhand

Cover design by Pas Niratbhand
Inside contents designed and produced by Greg Evans
Illustrations by Christian Paniagua

Copyright 2002 by Hangover Media, Inc.
ISBN: 1-931449-11-2

Printed in U.S.A.

CONTENTS

ACKNOWLEDGEMENTS

Huge bear hugs go to each of the 69 writers and researchers (their names and initials appear on the following page and their initials appear below the entries they worked on) who gave their blood, sweat, tears, and other bodily fluids to this project. Love taps to Christian Paniagua, our illustrator, and Greg Evans, our graphic designer, for contributing their creative juices. Thanks to all the great folks at Hangover Media for believing in this book and for making it a reality. A high five to "O", our superb editor, for caressing the text and making it purr. A pat on the back to my good buddy and recruiter extraordinaire, Alex Twersky, for his sound business advice and good—and bad—humor. Special thanks go to Helene Silver of City & Company, the publisher of the first edition of Erotic New York, for lending me her ear and good counsel.

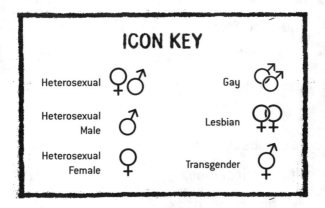

ABOUT THE AUTHOR

Tim Haft is the author of five books, including the first edition of *Erotic New York* (City & Company, 1998). In addition to having a knack for finding naughty nooks, Tim is the co-founder of Resume Deli (www.resumedeli.com), an online resume critiquing service: he is also a freelance edior and an ACE-certified personal trainer. You can reach him at haft2bfit@rcn.com.

WRITERS & RESEARCHERS

Rebecca Argyle (RA)

Melissa Rose Bernardo (MRB)

Melissa Bloom (MB)

Michael H. Broder (MHB)

Rachel Kramer Bussel (RKB)

Emilia Canahuati (EC)

Michele Capozzi (MC)

Nella Dawn Casalino (NDC)

Margaret Dean Cashill (MDC)

Robert Cashill (RC)

Su Ciampa (SC)

Daire Coco (DC)

Saskia Cornes (SCCC)

Bree Coven (BC)

Doreen Coppola (DCZ)

Katherine Darnell (KD)

Justin Deabler (JD)

Courtney Devon (CD)

Dina DiMaio (DD)

Kristen Edelmann (KE)

David Ernst (DE)

Lark Floresca (LF)

Kate Goehring (KG)

Jessica Goldbogen (JG)

Beth Goldstein (BG)

Diana Goldstein (DG)

Pamela Grossman (PG)

Tim Haft (TH)

Damian Hartner (DH)

Alexandra Harvey (AH)

Matt Heindl (MH)

Elaine Heinzman (EH)

Jens Hewerer (JH)

Marsha Johnson (MJ)

Angela Kozlowski (AK)

Mara Kushner (MK)

WRITERS & RESEARCHERS

Costanza Lamperti (CL)

Eli Lang (EL)

LéGray (LG)

Sheryl Ann Levart (SAL)

Vadim Lieberman (VL)

Sharon Lintz (SL)

Lei Liu (LL)

Tim Martin (TM)

Kimberly Maska (KM)

Gia Elisa Miller (GM)

Federica Moschella (FM)

Matt Nelko (MN)

Ndlela Nkobi (NN)

Mark O'Connell (MO)

Lindsay Pollock (LDP)

Tim Ranney (TR)

Sarah Safransky (SS)

Zarine Sagar (ZS)

Jason Schneiderman (JS)

Stephanie Schroeder (SES)

Rachel Sklar (RS)

Milton F. Stone (MFS)

Felicia Sullivan (FS)

Jean A. Tang (JAT)

Joey Terach (JT)

Yolanda Thomas (YT)

Hannah Tinti (HT)

Lateefah Torrence (LT)

Tristan Trout,
   CorporateMofo.com (TT)

Alex Twersky (AT)

Melissa Ulto (MU)

Colleen Vincent (CV)

Heather Wedl (HW)

INTRODUCTION:
Erotic New York

EROTIC AND NEW YORK GO TOGETHER LIKE LOX and bagels, Laurel and Hardy, Tom and Jerry—well you get the idea. In this "city that never sleeps," every fetish, sexual orientation, and erotic practice is not just tolerated, but welcomed and embraced. What other city has hosted an erotica expo in their state-funded convention center?

Granted, city government has spurred efforts in recent years to "Disneyfy" the Times Square area and eradicate the more visible purveyors of adult entertainment from residential neighborhoods, but this has done virtually nothing to dampen the spirit of Eros that has always pervaded the Big Apple.

This second edition of *Erotic New York* has been painstakingly compiled by a team of 69 (really!) randy writers and researchers who scoured the city for Gotham's most titillating treats. Their mission: to help you discover "the best sex in the city," whether you're straight, gay, lesbian, bi, transgender, male, female, single, in a committed relationship, married, polyamorous, or someplace in between. *Erotic New York* will introduce you to a sizzling world of sex-citing possibilities from bawdy baths to bodacious bars, torrid tattoos to tantalizing toys, sensual stripping to shameless swinging, delightful domination to decadent dancing, and so much more. For quick and dirty navigation, the book is organized by "vice" and at the back you'll find handy indexes, including one by neighborhood, to help you quickly locate the sexual delights closest to home.

Because our goal is to help you—the erotic explorer—find fun, fulfillment, and satisfaction on your carnal quest, our reviewers tell it like it is. They include their own highly personal experiences and on occasion get down and dirty with x-rated descriptions, so consider yourself forewarned.

Bear in mind that it's not unusual for businesses—especially of the adult variety—to close, relocate, or change their hours, policies, and/or prices, so be sure to call ahead before venturing out. We'd hate for you to get caught with your pants down.

Now it's time to lie back, spread your legs, and get ready to discover that ceaselessly pulsating, aphrodisiacal den of iniquity known as *Erotic New York*.

Play hard, but play safe
The Erotic New York Team

BAWDY BARS & NIGHT-CLUBS

BETWEEN 9 AND 5, AND OFTEN MUCH, MUCH LATER THAN that, most New Yorkers are all about business—aggressively scaling their chosen career ladder with all the energy and zeal of the Tasmanian devil. But once the sun goes down, these same folks rapidly shift into play mode, and their concerns about mergers, acquisitions, revenue, and ratings no longer seem so earth shattering. Instead, the denizens of Gotham begin to focus on the horizontal tango, doin' the nasty, and other delights of the flesh. The untamed sexual beast emerges as though a full moon were permanently parked over Manhattan. Dance clubs pulse, DJs spin, lights flash, dancers gyrate, shots are swallowed, and lovers embrace into the obscene hours as the city builds toward one big collective orgasm. Then the sun rises and the whole cycle starts all over again. Gee, this is a fun place.

The average New York City bar or nightclub is all about music, dancing, drinking, and conversation, but we know you're not interested in an average night out. Here we've listed some of the steamiest nightspots where the touch of Eros is readily apparent. For maximum enjoyment, dress sharp (you can't go wrong with head to toe black), and arrive late—many clubs don't start hopping until well after midnight. And when planning to visit a club, be sure to call ahead, as parties and theme nights constantly shift days and venues. *—TH*

Bar d'O

29 Bedford at Downing Street
212-627-1580
M-Su: 6-close
Happy hour: M-F 6pm-8pm
Call for show times and cover charge (usually $5)

DON'T GET THE WRONG IMPRESSION FROM BAR d'O's slightly seedy exterior. Inside, this cozy, intimate bar is all class and sass. The Euro crowd is sexy young and hip, and the earth-toned décor is striking, with lots of comfy couches. The lighting from red vulva-esque sconces makes the high-end crowd look like a million dollars.

Modeled after a French cabaret, Bar d'O asks that you keep your feet in check (i.e., no dancing), as they don't have a cabaret license. But what they do have, after eight years on the scene, is some of the top drag talent in the city, including Lady Bunny and Cherry Vine. We saw house performers Miss Cachetta and Raven-O belt out standards from Duke Ellington, Ella Fitzgerald, Etta James, and Billie Holiday as well as country classics and good old, pop power ballads, well worth the reasonable cover charge. If men in kimonos, garters, glossy lips, and wigs are your thing, bring a napkin so you can clean up after yourself.

The attractive, youthful, well-dressed crowd is mixed—gay/straight and male/female. Monday night is the lesbian bash—$3 for girls, $5 for guys—but you better hang an X-chromosome from each hand if you want a taste of this womyn-for-womyn party. It's a safe place to bring your "straight" friends who need a little nudge out of the closet.

Although low on the cruise-o-meter, Bar d'O is a fun, fabulously entertaining place that seems best suited to couples. A single could pick up something nice at Bar d'O, but nice things are expensive, so don't leave home without your $50 line. —JD/MO

Blu

161 West 23rd Street between 6th and 7th Avenues
212-633-6113
M-Th: 4pm-4am; F-Sa: 4pm-8am

THIS "CHELSEA ORIGINAL" CERTAINLY LIVES UP to its name—design-wise that is. The thrust of the decor is, what else, blue—deep-to-medium blue everywhere punctuated by techno murals. But you have to squint to see it, given the dim lighting and smoky atmosphere.

Along with spirits and soda, the front bar is stocked with buff and chiseled bartenders. Sofas and arcade machines give way to an open area with a pool table. Further back is a small dance floor.

Blu features cutting edge DJs every night bolstered by a newly revamped sound system. The deafening volume of the usual thunka-thunka-variety club music will be uncomfortable for anyone who values his hearing. The nightly go-go boys dancing atop the pool table are, however, pure eye candy, helping to distract you from any potential long-term damage you might be inflicting on your inner ear.

The restroom facilities are decent—if you don't mind walking through a twisting, dark corridor, Helen Keller-style, groping your way to and from the dance floor.

The standard Chelsea crowd at Blu is salted with bridge-and-tunnel queens and older folk. Bring your atti-

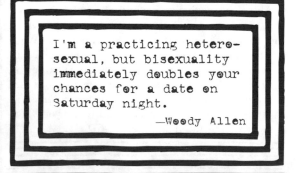

I'm a practicing hetero-
sexual, but bisexuality
immediately doubles your
chances for a date on
Saturday night.

—Woody Allen

tude and pray that your Prada whatever is this season's model. Take advantage of the two-for-one happy hour each night from 4pm-9pm. —*MJN*

Centro-Fly
51 West 21st Street between 5th and 6th Avenues
212-627-7770
www.centro-fly.com

MIRRORED BARS, WHITE LEATHER BANQUETTES, and sunken lounges covered in shag carpeting—pure kitsch ecstasy. Let the black and white ceiling hypnotize you into orgasmic euphoria. Centro-Fly's mod décor screams '60s, when orgy clubs were all the rage. While there's no open sex here, there are plenty of spectacles to get your undies in a frenzy. The music and dance floor alone is enough to get you off.

The best night for the beats is Friday, with the Great British House party hosted by DJ Penelope Tuesday, spiced up with visuals, dancers, and the occasional glimpse of Ms. Tuesday's breasts. If pounding music and hot bodies aren't enough to turn you on, then stripteases by Sophie Lamar and Amanda Lepore, two of the finest drag queens alive, are sure to tickle your fancy. And if you're still not ready to jump someone, well then there's always Viagra.

This club is without a doubt the "centro" of the New York City scene, featuring a super hi-tech sound system and lineup of internationally renowned DJs. While Centro-Fly holds the status of a club, it maintains the intimacy of a lounge courtesy of its two smaller rooms, Tapioca and Pinky, where aphrodisiacal temptations such as champagne oysters and chocolate fondue are served. So do as the flyest of the fly advise and "surrender yourself to music, sex, money, and pleasure." —*CD*

Clit Club in Exile: Tuff Titty at B-Bar

40 East 4th Street at Bowery (use Bowery entrance)
212-475-2220
Fridays: 10pm-4am
No cover, use password: Sassy
girlnightinNYC@hotmail.com

BACK IN 1990, LESBIAN DANCER/CHOREOGRAPHER Julie Tolentino invented something totally new, and she called it the Clit Club. The groundbreaking dyke-night out concept rode the sex-positive wave of the early 90s and provided a place where women could get down and get it on without apology or niceties. Fierce, sexy, and shakin', the old Clit Club achieved legendary status. It was the place to be on a Friday night. Shocking in its day, the dim, sleazy lower floor featured nonstop lesbian porn playing above the pool table while broad butches enveloped in leather stroked their pool sticks suggestively when sweaty women's studies majors in heavy eyeliner wandered down to cruise for a bathroom hook-up. Upstairs, nearly naked real dyke dancers pounded the stage, and there was even a go-go butch or two. The original Clit Club was so packed, you had to brush nipples with twenty women just to get to the coat check, which was all part of the plan. Glistening women threw their bodies about with abandon and mingled tongues and limbs with chicks whose names they never got. I remember a New Year's party where clothing was optional, candles were provided, and unscheduled live lesbian sex took place in many a corner. It was the closest thing lesbians had to a sex club. Clit Club was revolutionary, and hot as anything. So, what happened?

After nearly ten years, the Clit Club lost its space at Mother, that den of delicious iniquity in the Meatpacking District. Evicted but still determined, Clit Club soldiered bravely on to Flamingo, where it kept the go-go dancers and the dirty-danceable music, but lost just a bit of its edge. Now once more, Clit Club's been forced out of its home, and since November, Clit Club in Exile struggles to keep the spirit alive in a dramatically different space: the upscale restaurant B-Bar.

Renamed Tuff Titty, and billed as a mixed girl/boy party, it's now a good place to go if you've got your gay boyfriends in tow—there's some eye candy for them, too. The drinks are fantastic, but keep in mind that if you want to send something pink and frothy down to a pretty lady,

BOTTOMS UP:
New York City Cocktails

SEX AND ALCOHOL—SURE, YOU CAN ENJOY ONE without the other, but as any hard-grooving barfly would ask, why settle for less? Simply put, a drink or two can moisten your pucker, shake away inhibitions, calm the frayed edges of the psyche, and lay down a foundation for major debauchery—at least in your head.

And tastewise, the quintessential New York City cocktail should not be missed. "Sexy drink" no longer refers to the tropical fluorescence of a Sex on the Beach, or the liquorish linger of a clever mnemonic like a Sloe Comfortable Screw Against The Wall. These have been subsumed by innovations of the city's best mixologists, and passed on, via popular stylists, to national TV audiences eager to emulate trends introduced by the cast of shows like "Sex and the City." Nowadays, city denizens in-the-know pony up to flavored-vodka bars, down champagne cocktails such as the bellini—bubbly infused with peach nectar—and order cosmopolitans—a double-punch of vodka and triple sec, sweetened with Rose's Lime and prettied with a dash of cranberry juice—by the stainless splashback yard.

Sexy? You bet. Looking like a parade of pink stilettos, cosmopolitans and their progeny (Metropolitans, Manhattans, and countless other variations) are typically served "up" in long-stemmed martini glasses to the kinds of patrons who welcome any opportunity to bare their midriffs, even in mid-winter. Popular

it's gonna cost you (which is why it's a good thing there's no cover). B-Bar is ideally suited for the independently wealthy alcoholic. That said, it is one of the classier joints in town to host a girl's night, on par with uptown Julie's, which, while perhaps a good place to score a sugar mama, is not exactly erotic. But that's the problem. Neither is Clit Club anymore.

A concerted effort is made to coax the restaurant into a lesbo lounge (I can imagine a staffer frantically putting

spots—and hunting grounds—abound. For martinis, Pravda in Soho (281 Lafayette Street between Houston and Prince Streets; 212-226-4944), made mysterious and more Russian by the thickness of the cigar smoke, is famous for its green apple and cocoa-dusted chocolate martinis. Or, if you have money to burn, the round leather booths at the Royalton Hotel's "44" (44 West 44th Street between 5th and 6th Avenues; 212-944-8844) offer secluded grounds for smooching, and more (if you dare). Deep in the heart of Chelsea, the Viceroy (160 Eighth Avenue at 18th Street; 212-633-8484) mixes potent frozen cosmopolitans—stiff in more ways than one—and well-blended bellinis that can easily substitute for dessert. Or, take a date and be mesmerized by the handmade performance mixing at Angel's Share (8 Stuyvesant Street between 3rd Avenue and 9th Street). And for the latest aphrodisiac, try the elderflower champagne cocktails at the Bryant Park Hotel's Cellar Bar (40 West 40th Street between 5th and 6th Avenues; 212-642-2260).

Too much forbidden fruit? There's no such thing. And if you're in doubt, just remember what that eminent defender of decadence, W.C. Fields, once said: "Water? Never touch the stuff. Fish fuck in it." —*JAT*

up all those sapphic photos early Friday evening and then scampering to take them down in the wee hours of Saturday morning), but it's clearly an in-between, borrowed space. Exile isn't really the appropriate word. "Clit Club in limbo" is more like it.

DJs Ian and Shu ("both boys," one dyke sniffed) play a predictable one-level list that never really gets going, and gone are the go-go babes of yore. A few hot girls did jump on top of a riser to give their all, but the vibe was more basement party than hot girls' night out, and the action was neither tuff nor clitty. Basically a visit to Tuff Titty: Clit Club in Exile is an homage to an old gray mare that ain't what she used to be. Yet Clit Club is a living piece of dyke history and herotica. If she doesn't quite live up to her legendary wild youth, it's forgivable—after all, do any of us?   —BC

The Cock
188 Avenue A at 12th Street
212-627-1580
Daily: 10pm-close
F-Sa: $5; M-Th, Su: $3

WE HEARD THE WEEKEND CROWD AT THE COCK was mainly out-of-towners, but when we rolled in on Saturday at 1am, the only question on our minds was how these vacation birds smuggled so much metal and studded leather through airport security. In the three years since it opened, The Cock has lived up to every inch of its slimy rep—seedy, dark, and skintimate, something like a parking garage for Hyundais.

The real pull to The Cock is its Sunday night free-for-all in the notorious back room. We took the plunge one Saturday after midnight, and found a level of sexual vibe rivaled only by a junior high sex-segregated prom. Men sit and lurk in hungry solitude by the four benches along the wall, but the talk, touching, and sucking one would expect must have left the building before we arrived. Justin struck up an interesting, but un-erotic, conversation about photography with a new transplant to the city. Mark tested the bench waters with a coy grin, but the ocean currents in the back room were more likely to deliver Flipper than the meaty Jaws we hoped for when we crossed the dark threshold.

The Cock promises live entertainment, played out on a circular "stage," which is just a wee bit larger than the hamburger bun on a next-generation McDonald's entrée. Throw some quotes around "live," too, because those go-go dancers appeared to be sleepwalking on the bun, not that The Cock ever promised Gypsy Rose Lee or Liza. It's just that the dancers are surfing the same plane of consciousness as most of the patrons: drunk, high, or indifferent.

All this is to say that The Cock is a great time when you're in the mood, sort of like the greasy breakfast you crave when you're hungover. —JD/MO

Club Edelweiss

578 11th Avenue at 43rd Street
212-629-1021   ♂
Daily: 7pm-6am

DON'T GO TO EDELWEISS EXPECTING A SOUND OF Music theme bar. Though you may catch a patron in lederhosen, Club Edelweiss is definitely not fun for the entire family. It's neither small nor bright nor clean nor white, but they'll surely be happy to meet you—if you've got $30 for the cover, $8 for a drink, and whatever other sum may be required for "other" entertainment.

As trannie bars go, Club Edelweiss is fairly low profile. It's situated in a nowhere location; many of the plainly dressed, unassuming patrons nurse drinks all by their lonesome; and the shadowy corners in the basement are almost big enough to permit undetected nookie. But the transvestites strutting their stuff inside the club are anything but low-key. You'll see them flashing their sleek legs in stiletto heels and you'll also notice the absence of their packages (the crowd is a mixture of pre-and post-op, as well as your garden-variety scotch-tape users). Shiny black leather, metal accoutrements, and lots of exposed skin are the norm for the trannies, many of whom are looking for customers, not soul mates.

There are two levels to Club Edelweiss, and, conveniently, two exits. Outside, there is a velvet rope, but no line; and though a small card in the window does advise patrons to dress appropriately, neither of the two bouncers (of indeterminate sex) seemed to be enforcing any discernible standard. Expect to pay a cover, though the quoted $30 price is somewhat negotiable (men won't get away with less than $20, though).

Upstairs there are two bars and two large video monitors, which set the mood by showing explicit trannie porn. Black walls are highlighted with omnipresent neon, and there are a number of mirrored panels allowing for surreptitious scoping. The narrow front section opens into a spacious back room with minimal seating and a few bar tables. The beat is standard dance-club fare, which provides an appropriate backdrop for primping trannies, who cross and re-cross the floor as the solitary patrons pretend not to watch.

Downstairs provides a different experience. The beat in this netherworld is frenzied, the clientele uninhibited (certainly the bare chested bartenders were). There is a catwalk in the middle of the room, and it doesn't take long before lovely and lady-like patrons are on it, posing as the DJ recites their vitals. The vibe is more interactive, the eye contact more aggressive, and eventually the shadowy corners and shady spaces are put to good use by guests getting better acquainted.

But Club Edelweiss can only guarantee opportunity, not fulfillment—you close your own deals here. Patrons hoping for a little liquid courage shouldn't expect a huge selection—the bar is bare-bones, with draught beer, red wine, and a few basic mixers (don't stray too far from the coke; vodka and soda was a big production). The aforementioned deals are closed by the trannies, who have all the power here—they're better dressed, more confident, and in their element. The demographic is mixed, with almost exclusively black or Latino trannies and an across-the-board sample of customers, typically male and north of thirty. Toss in a few fetishists and the mix is complete—what happens next is up to you. Under the flashing lights of Club Edelweiss, that could be anything. —RS/DE

Coyote Ugly
153 1st Avenue between 9th and 10th Streets
212-477-4431
M-Th: 2pm-4am; F-Su: 12:30pm-4am
www.coyoteuglysaloon.com

♀♂

COYOTE UGLY SUCCESSFULLY UNITES UNBRIDLED sexuality and rampant alcoholism in that all-important window between drink-driven lust and vomitous regret. The ideal setting for a bachelor or bachelorette party, the lucky bride- or groom-to-be can be assured of enough photo ops to sustain future divorce proceedings. Exhibit one: the picture of Frank with his head comfortably nestled between the bartender's thighs while she drools a swig of tequila into his mouth. Or perhaps that shot of Linda drunkenly hinting at latent tendencies by crunching groin on the bar with her best friend from the office.

The women who staff the bar are consummate professionals. Unfailingly enthusiastic and clearly keen students of Flashdance, they navigate the bar with graceful dexterity. The sexuality feels contrived rather than erotic, but this is a venue that has more in common with the pragmatics of porn than first-date seduction. This ain't necessarily a bad thing in these tough economic times as those game enough to shake a bit of bar booty have been known to pocket some dollars in tips. Extra drinking money aside, the combined effects of cheap wine, an indeterminate number of cocksucking cowboys, and a crowd slurring loudly to "Jack and Diane" makes the urge to dance on the bar as irresistible as that hunky accountant leering at you from the corner.

The dress code for women consists of skin-hugging jeans and a black-cropped singlet. Accessorize with flicked blonde hair and you're off to a flying start. The men who frequent Coyote Ugly appear to have a sense of where the evening will leave them, and sport what would have to be the most undesirable, and clearly disposable, items in anyone's wardrobe.

For those wishing to get in a little practice dancing at the bar, the weeknight crowds are small and non-threatening. For the full experience, pencil Coyote Ugly in for a Friday or Saturday where it should—and probably will—be the final destination on your evening's itinerary. —SS

Crazy Nanny's

21 7th Avenue South at Leroy Street
212-366-6312
M-F: 4pm-4am; Sa-Su: 3pm-4am
F-Sa: $8 for women, $10 for men; no cover M-Th
Happy Hour: 4pm-7pm daily with half price drinks
www.crazynannys.com

LIKE YOUR OLD FAITHFUL HITACHI MAGIC WAND, women-owned Nanny's is always there, always ready, and always does the trick. Sure some newer models may be shinier, trendier, or a tad more glitzy, but Nanny's is a sure thing: a good old-fashioned lesbian bar and dance club that's refreshingly down to earth. It's reliable and a perfect first stop or break-in bar for the newly out, the just off work, or the chick who simply wants to get out (and get off) without confronting a lot of attitude.

Nothing's changed much at Nanny's since it opened in 1990 and that's part of what I like about it. The once telltale lavender building is now a burnt orange, and these days they card like crazy, but the walls are still lined with the same early '90s girl art of women straddling motorcycles and the occasional stray nipple pointed toward the sun. And they still play Rob Base rapping "It Takes Two." You'll find the requisite dyke pool table here and tournaments are held every Monday night. Karaoke is the big draw twice a week (Wednesday and Sunday) and there's even a newly instituted bingo night, but Friday is hands-down the night to go when things heat up for a party aptly named Sweat.

On Friday nights, this friendly neighborhood bar gets down and dirty. There's nothing quite like getting sweaty with strangers. "Will you wipe my back?" one flashy fox flirted at me, as I happily obliged, taking my time running the napkin between her shoulders. Legendary DJ MK (who recently had a stint on Rap City's Tha Bassment on B.E.T.) and Kim B spin house, r & b, calypso, reggae, and classics while a feast of B-girls, curvy spandex femmes, and women decked out in do rags, baseball shirts, and rainbow bandanas moved their hips, but it was all foreplay until the arrival of Lady Godiva—an erotic dancer who just may be the best kept secret in town.

Baby-faced and bootylicious, Lady Godiva treated the crowd to her signature butt shake from atop a little black box. No professional distance here, girls, Godiva's dance is an interactive experience. More than once I saw her reach into a patron's glitter tank top to release a full breast from a black satin bra, which she promptly took into her mouth with a grin. The truly lucky were up front when she dipped a finger into her shaved pussy (yes, we could see) and offered it around for a sniff. She good-naturedly accepted a smack on the ass and ground her butt into an eager face. A friend in the crowd remarked, "She loves it up there and it shows" as the singles turned to twenties— five of 'em—dotting the orange string that tied her up like a little present.

Dance at Crazy Nanny's and you won't dance alone. The crowd is friendly and approachable. Very popular with lesbians of color, Nanny's stays true to its tagline: "A place for gay women, biological or otherwise." Unofficial word has it that if you're a boy-girl couple looking for a third, Nanny's is one of the few lesbian bars where you won't get laughed at or thrown out on your ear.

Ignore the trendier-than-thou naysayers who tend to overlook the place, and disregard anything you may have heard about a rep for toughness. Nanny's is a solid choice. The very butch bartender upstairs (a regular for seven years) is reason enough to hightail it over. Oh, and don't forget to pick up your complimentary package of brightly colored dental dams on your way out the door. —BC

Dick's Bar
192 2nd Avenue at 12th Street
212-475-2071
Daily: 2pm-4am

DICKS. IF THAT'S WHAT YOU'RE LOOKING FOR, head to this neighborhood bar trafficked by men whose sticks are set to cruise control. Upon entering this small space, you'll find what at first seems like an innocent watering hole catering to guys in their late 20s and early 30s. But looks can be deceiving. Dick's is really a place to shop for…well…dicks. In fact, a grocery cart hangs from the ceiling near the entrance to remind you of your mission. And there's always a special on unpretentious, dressed-down, laid-back men.

Your shopping excursion begins at the bar area, where cheap drinks compensate for an indifferent staff. After a few vodka shots ($4 each), you've at least got an excuse to play a few cheesy '80s songs on the jukebox. The farther back you stroll in the narrow space, the cruisier it gets. At the end of the aisle, you'll discover a few arcade games and men playing with balls—oh wait, it's just a game of pool. Just as you grab a cue to challenge some hunk to a game, and use your intoxicated condition as an excuse for mishandling your pole, you notice the door to the bathroom. Shopping was never this much fun, you think to yourself, as you observe the cruisiest section of the bar. Should you see what's on sale inside? Well, that all depends on how much the vodka has dulled your senses!

Red lights cast an eerie glow throughout the bar, which gets more cramped with East Village locals as the night progresses. Mondays come alive with show tunes and Tuesdays and Thursdays are porn nights, with erotic videos playing on the bar's monitor to further whet your appetite. So whether you're starving for some tender beef

or some tasty fruit, the only currency you'll need at Dick's to make a purchase is a friendly attitude. —*VL*

Escuelita

301 West 39th Street between 8th and 9th Avenues
212-631 0588
Th-Sa: 10pm-5am; Su: 7pm-4am
Thursday: $5; Friday: $10; Saturday: $15; Sunday: $5 until 10pm, $8 after ($3 off admission with printout from website anytime except Thursday and Sunday 7pm-10pm)
www.escuelita.com

ESCUELITA IS A GAY BAR AND DANCE CLUB CATER-ing to a black and Latino crowd and featuring super buff (and extremely well hung) go-go boys and the best drag shows in town. The club is comfortable for lesbians, straight singles and couples, and gay men on the DL (down low). There are two bars (one with a drag queen waitress in a towering, butterfly-adorned flamingo pink wig), a dance floor, and bistro tables in a very dark space with lots of disco balls, strobe lights, and dry ice. The coat check line is long and slow moving, and the cost is $3 per item, so you might want to wrap your sweater around your waist or dump your stuff on a chair where a friend can keep an eye on it while sipping a drink and watching the action.

The music—an amalgam of salsa, merengue, bachata, R&B, hip-hop, classics, and house—is very loud, with the base mixed so high you can feel it pulsing through your body. This makes for a hypnotic wave of sound and sensa-tion highly conducive to dancing for hours on end, but not for chatting with cute boys. We're not saying it's impossi-ble to hook up here, just that it's mostly about the dancing and you'll probably get farther with body language than clever banter. But even if it's not the cruisiest club, it's total-ly worth it for the music, the drag shows, and especially for the go-go boys—sleek, buff, horse-hung, they dance like maniacs and sport hard-ons all night long while brothers slip dollar bills into their scanty loin coverings. Totally hot! Call for dinner reservations and event info. —*JS/MHB*

Heaven

579 6th Avenue at 16th Street
212-539-3982
Friday: 5pm–4am; Sunday: 5pm–midnight
Friday: $10 after 7pm; Sunday: $5
girlclubevent@aol.com

GIRL CLUB PRODUCTIONS PRESENTS TWO PARTIES at Heaven: Kaliedoscope Friday and Fantasy Sunday. The former is dedicated to "all nations, all colours, all women," and producers, Sue Martino and Nicole Parker, mean it. They intend to have the Friday night party mixed to the max. This gay-owned multilevel, multicultural facility is divided into heaven, purgatory, and hell—three floors of hot, steamy fun for lesbians and their friends.

At Kaliedoscope Friday, the first floor is filled with dancers percolating to classics, Top 40 tunes, '70s, '80s, and dance hits. On the second floor, salsa, merengue, bachata, cumbia, house, R&B, reggae, and soul rule. Both floors have long, elegant bars with beautiful and attentive bartenders—"Fallen Angels," according to Heaven's promotional literature. Exotic dancers, featuring the spicy Ousha and her girls, light up the first floor stage with a tantalizing and erotic go-go show. The performers ride the poles on stage, dance on the bar, mix with the crowd, and indulge in the occasional lap dace while voyeurs stuff dollar bills in their skimpy, sexy outfits.

Fantasy Sunday makes for a terrific post-brunch stop—drinks are just half price from five to six and the crowd is a winner. I encountered a few lovelies at the bar early in the evening and had pleasant conversations and free drinks. Try an Absolut Citron martini—it sets you up for just the right dancing buzz. After imbibing, head up to the fetish show on the third floor where mistresses

Erotica, Mia, Maine, and Katherine model the latest fetish fashions. You can also play, cruise, and dance here with both the young and the young at heart. DJ Tanco spins titillating tunes for the pleasure of all the girls.

I'd have to concur with Ms. Parker's description of Heaven: "Three floors of fine looking women." The third floor is also available for private parties—a beautiful layout and eager producers will make your party sparkle and shine. —*SES*

Hogs & Heifers

1843 1st Avenue between 95th and 96th Streets
212-722-8635
Tu-Th: 3pm-3am; F-Sa: 4pm-4am
www.hogsandheifers.com

♀♂

IF YOU LIKE YOUR BARS A LITTLE ROUGH AROUND the edges and have a penchant for bras (check out the growing collection behind the bar), you'll like Hogs and Heifers. Ignore the fact that Hogs is on the Upper East Side—this is not your typical post-fraternity house establishment and, in fact, is vastly superior to its West Village sister (859 Washington St.; 212-929-0655) of the same name (it's much bigger too!). Live music is the main attraction here. Six nights a week, with shows typically starting at 9:30pm, various bands take to the stage, playing rock, blues, and country. Tuesday features a blues jam during which anybody who can play an instrument is welcome to shamelessly strut his stuff onstage.

The tough and sexy bikini-clad barmaids, armed with bullhorns, pour a mean drink and stomp around showing off their well-toned midriffs. Look at them the wrong way and before you know it you'll have the imprint of a cowboy boot on your butt. The bar is a haven for men who want to hang out with their own kind, toss back some shots (no wine is served), listen to live music, and shoot some pool. According to our in-the-know bartender, Hogs and Heifers is also the best place in the city for women to meet hot men—the kind of guys who lack the pretension that runs rampant in other, cleaner hangouts. In fact, she was quite right. Within five minutes, we were swarmed over by a crowd of men that were more than eager to make our acquaintance. —*KD/FS*

Lips

2 Bank Street at Greenwich Avenue
212-675-7710
M-Th, Su: 5:30-midnight; F-Sa: 5:30-1am;
Sunday brunch: 11:30am-4:30pm
www.lipsnyc.com

IF MARTHA STEWART WALKED INTO LIPS, SHE might just have a heart attack. This drag cabaret/restaurant (Italian cuisine with entrees ranging from $12 to $22) would likely win the award for the tackiest décor in the city. In the upstairs dining room, disco balls and chandeliers hang from the ceiling, and the walls, adorned with fake jewels, are painted bright shades of pink, purple, and green. Not to be outdone, the drag-queen wait staff blends in perfectly with its gaudy attire.

The performers, who are none other than your friendly waitresses, take the stage at 7pm and perform until closing time. On the night we visited, there were a smattering of private celebrations going on, and indeed, the restaurant seems well suited for a birthday or bachelorette party. If you happen to be the guest of honor, be forewarned, there is no escaping public humiliation. But don't worry too much, as the acts are fairly tame. After your moment of glory, the wait staff will be delighted to preserve your embarrassment for posterity by snapping some Polaroids of you in various compromising positions. And when it comes time to make that birthday wish, don't be surprised if your cake—and candle—mysteriously find their way between the legs of your server. And yes, in order to get your dessert, you must blow.

In the downstairs bar you can watch more drag queens as they lip synch old favorites like "Tits and Ass" from *A*

Chorus Line. As expected, members of the audience are a big part of the act. A little friendly touching and teasing is de rigueur for each show, but the performers don't go for the jugular, and if you're a good sport, you might even leave with a few new beauty tips. One drag queen who took a liking to us and noticed our small breasts (bitch!), suggested we place rice in an old pair of pantyhose and then stuff the hose into our bras for a realistic, enhanced look. And you know what ladies, it actually works! —*GM*

Lovergirl at True
28 East 23rd Street between Broadway and Park Avenue South
212-254-6117
Sa: 10pm-4am
$8 before midnight; $10 after (see website for details and membership discounts)
www.lovergirlnyc.com

LOVERGIRL BILLS ITSELF AS "NEW YORK'S HOTTEST dance party for women," and they've got the goods to back it up.

If the go-go girls dancing in a cage don't do it for you, how 'bout a girl-on-girl lap dance from the deceptively named Angel Baby, who makes it pretty clear she's into girls by the way she moves? Put it this way: it doesn't look like work. The gorgeous and talented femme fatale will work you over for around $10 to $15, but believe me, you'll want to give her more.

A staple of the scene for five years now, Lovergirl is celebrating its two-year anniversary at True, the sexy nightclub host to "alternative" weekly parties such as Gomorrah and Kitsch-Inn. But on Saturday nights, it's all about the ladies, and nearly 300 women rush to check each other out upon arrival. The upstairs bar offers cozy make-out couches, elevated for the exhibitionistic; a wide open dance floor; and a stage where beautiful and professionally trained dancers—

like local favorite go-go goddess Maine (seen on MTV)—strut their stuff to the adulation of a panting crowd.

Two DJs on two floors, Steven "Chip Chop" Gonzales and Mary Mac, promise a mix of house, Latin house, tribal, salsa, hip-hop, funk, r & b, and reggae, but it doesn't stop there. There's something subversive about dykes pinning each other against the wall and grinding to Britney Spears' "Slave 4 U." Whatever it is, it works, especially when you descend a deep red staircase to the sexy downstairs Mac's Lounge, which sets the perfect stage for all those mack daddies (masculine and sexually aggressive dykes). Dark and throbbing, the lower lounge has the

Hot Rock

CALLING ALL PYROS, PERVS, SLUTS, AND FREAKS who like to play with fire. Check out Torch Job, Gotham's very own rabble-rousers and fetish rockers. Set to the incendiary sounds of noise punk with deliciously lewd lyrics about girl on girl action and what happens when truckers mess with bad ass girls on the road, the trio that make up Torch Job like to blow things up and the audience seems to dig their onstage antics. Featuring Tara Fire Ball, bass player and pyrotechnic sculptress, Samantha the Pantha on drums and Rex The Sex Machine (often mistaken for one of the girls when wearing a skirt) on axe guitar, each member of this powerful ménage a twat storms the stage dressed only in electrical tape or tutus, treating the audience to an excessive display of decadence, danger, and debauchery. To see what lascivious tricks Torch Job has up their sleeves or to sign on to their email list go to http://groups.yahoo.com/group/BaitnTackle/.

Another punk band gone erotic on the local scene is Licky. Lead vocalist Lips, joined by bandmates Sacky, Pool of Blood, and Moby (not the original electronic musician and animal rights guru) stir up a fast-paced assault of naughty songs like "Sometimes You Have to Pretend to be Gay to get some Pussay." Check out their mp3s on the web at http://artists3.iuma.com/IUMA/Bands/licky/. —AH

anonymous feel of a back room. You can rub up against a stranger with very little effort. The hip-swayin' beats got me in the mood. Fifteen minutes before last call, I danced up against a stranger's ass and wound up with a dinner invitation. Couldn't hear a word she said above the music, but as is often the case with these scenarios, it didn't matter. The sweet young thang and I made out against the bar until closing time when they gently pushed us outside.

Lovergirl is always reinventing itself and finding new ways to keep the party—and the girls—fresh. Past events include a kissing contest and a unique brand of star search with the chance to win a shot in the cage, an honor for which go-go virgins from the audience had to perform a lap dance for the dancers on stage. I hear the winner made some decent tips. A bit of a trendsetter on the scene, Lovergirl has featured everything from CD releases and giveaways (including Nellie Furtado, before anyone knew who she was) to drag king performances and a prescreening of Aleada Minton's docu-short "Butch Body Blues." Women's wrestling mania may be the next big thing. As club owner "Megaboy" Kate says, "Time Out called Lovergirl 'the lesbian go-go central.' I call it a lot of fun." None would dare to disagree. Lovergirl is definitely where the girls are. The eclectic, laid-back, and triple-x sexy crowd will keep you grooving. If you wanna get lucky on a hot first date, or you've got only one night on the town, make this the place. And smile at the door bois (boys). They're real nice. —*BC*

Lucky Cheng's

24 1st Avenue, between 1st and 2nd Streets
212-473-0516
Su-Th: 6pm-midnight; F-Sa: 6pm-2am (bar/lounge stay open later)
$15 minimum at tables; appetizers: $6-$10; entrees: $14-$21;
tarot readings: approximately $20

"HAPPY BLOW JOB TO YOU. HAPPY BLOW JOB TO you…" That's what you're likely to hear if you venture inside this Chinese restaurant/drag queen extravaganza on your birthday.

For a unique and memorable evening with a few of the city's most interesting waitresses, take your friends to Lucky Cheng's. The drag queens-cum-wait staff at this East Village, Asian-themed restaurant are always up for a little fun, not to mention seduction and some friendly molestation.

If we didn't know better we would have guessed that some of our servers really were female. "Are those breasts really fake?" we wondered to ourselves. Damn, these chicks have better bodies than most of the women we know, but alas, like many males, their fashion sense—or lack of it—was a dead giveaway. Fluorescent spandex miniskirts, and tacky tube tops were the order of the day.

Lucky Cheng's has two levels, both of which contain restaurants and bars. The cabaret shows are held upstairs in a blue and orange space where Japanese parasols, Asian lamps, and Chinese ornamental dragons hang from the ceiling. Downstairs there's a karaoke bar where you can perform for free, but don't be surprised if you get a quick boot from a drunken drag queen looking for her fifteen minutes of fame. During our visit, a bachelorette party was underway in this space. Two male customers had stripped to their underwear and were feeding the bachelorette bananas from their crotch. Not to be outdone, a staff member arrived with a much larger phallic symbol—a boa constrictor. A Polaroid of you, your date, and the boa is only $5.

Back upstairs, the audience consisted of a few birthday boys and girls, some bachelorettes, and one woman celebrating her hysterectomy. "We'll just celebrate putting all of your eggs in one basket," the host announced to the latter. Celebrants beware! You might be asked to take a shot of a white, creamy, alcoholic beverage—topped with a cherry, of course—straight from your waitress's mouth. And while you're ordering, don't be surprised if the waitress sits on your lap, grabs your breasts, and/or fondles your genitals. If you're really lucky, or unlucky as the case may be, you might be sent to the "drag box", sort of like the penalty box in hockey. There, in full view of all, you'll be serenaded, groped, rubbed upon, danced on, and molested. And ladies take our advice: don't wear a skirt!

Lucky Cheng's food is mediocre, but the entertainment is well worth the price. Drag your ultra-naïve friends with you (when they realize that these waitresses are really men, the looks are priceless) and be prepared for an evening of non-stop laughter and humiliation. —*GM*

Meow Mix

269 East Houston Street at Suffolk Street
212-254-0688
www.meowmixchix.com
Daily: 5pm-4am
$5 (men $10; must be accompanied by a woman)

TRUE TO ITS EAST VILLAGE ROOTS, MEOW MIX IS jumpin' with pierced, tattooed, lefty lesbos, for whom the bar has become an extended living room, a queer "*Cheers*," if you will. Twice proclaimed "Best Bar" by *Homo Xtra* magazine, Meow Mix is certainly the neighborhood bar of choice for the city's cool cats. Seen in the film *Chasing Amy*, and known for occasional celebrity drop-ins (from Kimberly Pierce to Ellen DeGeneres), by now Meow Mix is a little bit famous, as are its regular Xena nights and signature "Don't Fuck with the Ladies" T-shirts. But Thursday night is glamourpuss night at Meow Mix as the high femme fashionistas come out in full gear, gussied up for a party called "Gloss." Sassy, stylin' promoters Chloe and Rachael mean business when they say they've got the "glammest girlie night around."

A welcome, long overdue homage to femmes, this night gives the girly girls reason to dress up—and plenty of cuties to parade around for. I don't know how they do it, but they get the most gorgeous crowd including very young (if you're over 30 you'll feel ancient), nubile glamour dykes in glitter fishnets, turbo femmes with dangerous necklines, drag kings in cowboy hats, punk chicks, baby butches, trannie boys, and village hipsters—if you can't find your type here, you're not trying hard enough. No wonder lesbian sexpert and *Village Voice* columnist Tristan Taormino christened Gloss the "Best Cruising Night for Dykes," noting the high make-out success ratio.

On hand to put you in the mood are DJ Nina Skittles, playing glam '80s hits, followed by BK Brewster who doles out old school, hip-hop, and big beat. Go-Go Starlets entertain, featuring dyke go-go diva Maine, wrapped around the lucky pole in camouflage boy briefs, hanging upside down by her strong, sexy thighs. The night I went to get Glossed, the girls and I were privy to go-go girl auditions. Among the contenders were a curvy vixen in a latex bikini and a Lolita fantasy come to life—a petite princess in a pleated schoolgirl skirt. Everyone there either wanted to be her or do her, or—let's be honest here—both.

Speaking of honesty, three can crowd into a bathroom, and nobody counts how long you're in there. A group of us once played show or tell, and once when two girls were keeping it busy, I reached up under my little black mini right at the bar to pull down my tights and show off a new tattoo. It's not like nobody notices, but nobody minds. It's about as comfortable a cruising spot as it gets.

That said, it's mostly regulars at Gloss, so everyone already knows everyone. Best to go armed with a powder puff posse or make yourself a regular so you become one of the familiar lovely faces. With goods like this to ogle, you'll want to anyway. And, darlin', don't forget to dress up (it'll be more fun to undress later). —*BC*

◎◎ EROTIC

Monster

80 Grove Street at Sheridan Square
212-924-3557
M-F: 4pm-4am; Sa-Su: 2pm-4am (tea dance: M-Sa at 10pm; Su at 5:30pm)

MONSTER ENJOYS THE GAYEST, MOST HISTORIC OF locations, right across from the Stonewall Inn. Amble past the stone men-to-men and womyn-to-womyn sculptures in the triangular garden of Sheridan Square and you're practically in the lobby of the fantastic, old high-rise that houses the bar. It's the sort of place that you'd never connect with its name—those bright warm lights and open spirit don't seem to jibe with the beastly moniker. Dig beneath that warm exterior and you may find the easiest, most promising pick-up of your gay life.

We visited Monster during the holiday season, but the kitschy wise men and Christmas banners were practically lost among the rest of the trash-positive décor. The walls are plastered with old movie icons, divas of days past, and images of happy drunk patrons smiling for the camera.

We were surprised by the grand piano and the insistent belting of show tunes issuing from one corner. The whole bar was caught in a frenzy of songs from the *Little Shop of Horrors*, but the true horror was a pair of love handles and ankle boots pumping to "Down on Skid Row." From our perch behind the piano, we observed the staircase to the lower level. Could it be a dungeon on Sixth Avenue—the geographic destination of Eros for all these middle-aged queens and their youthful gay companions? Unfortunately not. To our dismay, the Monster's bowels only contained the women's restroom (men get to go at street level).

As an enormous birthday cake shot up the stairwell, we flew to the center of the action. "Free champagne and cake," one spindly, Asian boy crowed. And that was when we got a sense of the vibe: the Monster is truly one of the friendliest, most open gay spots we have ever come across. No wonder little queens and nancies parade in front of the Ensure-chugging crowd to cut their lavender teeth. This bodes well for the explorer seeking elusive C & A (cock and ass). If you don't mind a little potbelly, corduroy, or mismatched belt and shoes, The Monster seems to be the most hardcore, if unassuming, of pick-up joints. The eyes are friendly in their hunger, always confident that closing time will bring a new trick and few consequences. The place is mobbed most nights for good reason. While clubs like Twilo are busy catering to the high-maintenance, too strung-out-to-fuck crowd, the Monster quietly cultivates a clientele that knows exactly what it wants. So if you can manage to exorcise the melody of Suddenly Seymour during your cab ride home, you're good to go and the Monster has once again worked its West Village magic.   —*JD/MO*

Nowbar

22 7th Avenue South at Leroy Street
212-802-9502
Tu-Su: 10pm-4am
$15-$20 ($5 discount for girls, trannies, and those in drag)

As we approached Nowbar we were expecting another Bar d'O—a small funky lounge with decent cabaret acts, a mostly gay crowd, and the occasional queen—but what we got was completely different.

The club is dark and smoky with wet-look walls and funky lighting. The diverse crowd consisted of decked-out queens, celebrity look-alikes, straight folks into good dance music, cross-dressing lesbians, and the occasional Wall Street suit. Although there is no formal dress code at Nowbar, we suggest you hang your business casual on the office door and leave it there. Leather or feathers would be good choices.

If you prefer to be in the closet about your penchant

for wearing the clothes of the opposite sex, we were informed by one of the bartenders that there's a cross-dressing room—complete with lighted make-up mirrors—upstairs. That bit of info may come in handy if you choose to compete in one of the club's various cross-dressing contests; a hot one takes place at Gil T. Pleasure's weekly Thursday night fetish party.

At 11:30pm on a Friday evening the crowd had already

The Wau Wau Sisters

HE WAU WAU (PRONOUNCED "VOW-VOW," OR "Va-Vow") Sisters perform at Galapagos (70 North 6th St.; 718-782-5188), a converted warehouse, in bohemian Williamsburg, Brooklyn. Tanya and Adrienne (they are in fact sisters) perform a free show every Monday night, from 10pm-12:30am, from October through June. These twenty-something cuties entertain with a wide array of costume changes and acrobatics, all while strumming chic pink guitars and singing songs of sexual ambition and disillusionment.

The show, while sexy in a cute sort of way, is not exactly erotic. But that said, the sisters do favor frilly bikini bottoms, feather boas, sparkly tiaras, vanity muscle tops, and pink high heels. The costumes are dazzling and there are lots of them. The sisters first appear as natural brunettes, wearing pink and black "Rocker" baby T-shirts. As the evening progresses, they morph into platinum-haired birthday presents wearing nothing but large pink boxes and bows in their hair. In later sets, they dress up as diamond-white trapeze artists and, most strikingly, as members of the band Lynyrd Skynyrd. Accessories include silver dog collars and dolls of the plastic and inflatable variety. For a low- to no-budget production, the visual effects are impressive.

The sisters also impress with their limber bodies. The trapeze segment is a remarkable feat in which the two twirl around a single bar suspended from the ceiling of the crowded room. As they rotate around the bar, supporting each other by the ankles, the feathers fly and the room goes silent. At one point, they even appear to steal a kiss (incestuous fantasies, anyone?). Tanya, a Molly Shannon look-alike, demonstrates the most impressive gymnastic prowess, standing on her hands during an entire

filled the main space downstairs, necessitating the opening of the club's street-level space, usually reserved for private parties. We slithered through the crowd and sank into one of the booths that ring the bar. As on most Fridays, Diva '74 was holding court—think lots of disco, funk, and polyester. On other nights you might be serenaded by the sounds of techno, hip-hop, trance, or '80s hair bands. On the lower level, well-known drag and trannie performers

song (she isn't singing or playing guitar, however), and supporting Adrienne's weight while in a backbend for the duration of another song. The sets are short (15 minutes), and the time between them long (for the elaborate costume changes), but the wait is worth it.

Judging from the large, boisterous crowd of artists, hipsters, and former dot-commers that came out late on a Monday night, there's no doubt that the sisters have a cult following. As soon as they took the stage, the audience burst forth with song requests ("play Jezebel") and graphic catcalls. The sisters maintained a familiar, intimate connection with the spectators with their folksy—and at times—corny material. The lyrics are not always the most innovative: "A pinch of you/to put in my stew; A gallon of you/puts my car on the freeway," but they can get a little racy: "my pussy is dry and my panties are wet" The musical highlights were a lip-synched version of "Free Bird" accompanied by a striptease and a ballad-like version of Quiet Riot's "Cum On Feel the Noize."

The Wau Wau Sisters may never play Carnegie Hall, but their fans don't care. They just eat them up. As one friend said the night I saw them, "they're so bad, they're good, and that's really good," but then again, he had had quite a few drinks. Between sets, the girls and their boyfriends (and even their father) mingled with the audience, and at the end of the show, they emerged once again—to accept well-deserved donations (after all, it was a free show).

My new friends at the bar encouraged me to stay until the end of the show for a rhinestone-clad creature called the Bunny Man, which everyone agreed is beyond description. Unfortunately, he didn't show that night, guaranteeing that this writer will definitely return to see what all the fuss is about. —DG

were strutting their stuff. Most nights feature two to four performances (both cabaret and lip-sync). Saturday is Glorya Wholesome's Living Legends party, which features look-alike celebs.

If you haven't experienced trannie cabaret before, Nowbar is a good place to start. Come with an open mind and be ready to party because a night at Nowbar is anything but a drag! —*ZS*

Red

503 East 53rd Street between 1st and 2nd Avenues
212-688-1284
Daily: 6pm-4am

IT'S VERY SIMPLE: GUYS GO TO THE RED TO PICK up or be picked up. If a customer isn't an escort, dancer, masseuse or some kind of hustler, odds are, he has money to spend. Hooking up in bars seems to have become a hackneyed practice, trite and wearisome for the modern gay man. Red attempts to put some good ol' fun into the mix.

The bar lies behind an unmarked door in a row of bustling establishments on East 53rd Street. A narrow flight of carpeted stairs leads to a second door resembling the entrance to a private apartment. Red is a lot like a private party; the space is intimate and the patrons mingle like friends. The bar is to the right, tables are scattered throughout, and there's a small stage in back. Appropriately, the place is bathed in red lights.

The flyer boasting, "When you want it, you can find it," doesn't lie. Everyone's looking for action here. Early in the evening, a handful of men relax at the bar watching porn on the TV monitor. By the end of the night, the porn is all but ignored. The room gets hot and hedonistic! Music blares, testosterone flows; it's hard not to be sucked into the revelry.

Only two nights of the week, Wednesday and Monday, are without preplanned themes. On "Jimmie's Red Light Tuesday," the bar offers $3 cosmos (an incredible find in the city), until midnight. Patrons are invited to participate in nude body painting or to cheer on erotic dancers on the stage in back. Thursday's wild party features XX College Boy Model Search, hosted by eastsideboys.com, a local escort service. On Amateur Fridays, striptease virgins disrobe to Latin beats before a riotous crowd. Catch a bed show on Sinfest Saturdays and get a head start (no pun intended), on the new week with The Papi Party on Sunday night. Hosted by Big City Video, the party features porn premiers, video giveaways, and an opportunity to meet the stars.

Red welcomes customers every night of the week, catering primarily to the after-work crowd. For all the action that takes place here, it's unbelievable there's no cover, but it's true. Many cite the bar's middle-of-the-road status as its allure. Though a pick-up spot for hustlers, it's reminiscent of gay gentlemen's clubs of the '50s. So why stay at home when you can drink some beers, watch some porno, and maybe meet the man of your dreams?   —MDC

Red Rock West Saloon
457 West 17th Street at 10th Avenue
212-367-7395
Daily: noon-4am   ♀♂

ANOTHER BAR IN THE "COYOTE UGLY" MODE, the Red Rock West Saloon is a rowdy good time. It's essentially a white-trash roadhouse transported to the western fringe of Chelsea. The place attracts a fairly diverse crowd—from New Jersey suburbanites to members of the local chapter of Dykes on Bikes—all gathered to watch the extremely hot, rather scantily dressed barmaids get up on the bar and dance. Be forewarned: the bartenders have no reservations about pulling unsuspecting women from the crowd to shake their thangs alongside them, and boy do they shake it. This place can bring out the wild side of the wimpiest wallflower, and the jukebox—which features rowdy bands like AC/DC and Charlie Daniels—merely adds fuel to the fire.

The Red Rock has the standard assortment of beers (only moderately overpriced), but the real treat is getting a shot directly from a bartender's belly button! There are pool tables in back, though trying to play a game in this crowd would take the concentration of a Zen monk. You can also buy an assortment of official Red Rock West merchandise, which will no doubt prove a valuable memory aid the next morning, when you try to recall how you got that new tattoo.

The only killjoy here is the presence of the several very large bouncers strategically placed like lifeguards throughout the room. They watch the crowd as if they're just looking for an excuse to kick someone's ass. But, for those who like to get wild, or want to get someone else wild, and don't mind doing it under the surveillance of a bunch of guys who look like Hell's Angels doing a "Baywatch" impression, the Red Rock is a pretty safe bet. —*TT*

Remote Lounge
327 Bowery at 2nd Street
212-228-0228
Daily: 6 pm-4 am
Th-Sa after 10pm: $3-$5; free at other times

REMOTE LOUNGE, LOCATED IN THE HEART OF THE East Village behind tinted glass doors, provides entertainment that's tailored to the voyeurs among us. It's equipped with more than 80 cameras and lined with personal viewing booths furnished with joysticks that control the cameras. The viewing consoles—part video poker game, part *Buck Rogers* mission control and part Fisher-Price—are also equipped with phone receivers and paging systems for the ultimate in 21st century flirtation. There is even a "nurse" button: one push summons the cocktail waitress to your side.

From the privacy of your own table, take snapshots via your console of intriguing patrons lounging, flirting, and (often times) flashing or groping, and view the images in real time at www.remotelounge.com. As drinks pour and the clock nods past midnight, the electricity in the room nearly pricks your knickers and bursts of exhibitionism often erupt. Size up the bartender's rack or a stranger's bulge without guilt, catty looks, or black eyes!

Imagine *Temptation Island* or *Real World* party scenes, with no network censorship, meeting *Taxicab Confession*. In a mere three hours at Remote, this reviewer was scoped, trolled, cruised and abused by men and ladies alike—all from a mere fifteen feet away. Dysfunctional socializing? Maybe. However, the communication consoles swelled my balls enough to approach any lady in the house while at the same time padding my ego enough to enjoy cavesdropping on my date. High-fives, waves, winks, giggles and a few phone numbers were exchanged with fellow patrons as my party departed our booth and slid back into reality. The next morning I surfed up all the snapshots of the previous evening—talk about a visual rolodex. Who were these people? A few gin and tonics erased most of that, but I have a great glimpse into the mind's eye of the New York lounge set!

There's a good mix of people at Remote: some bra-less and ready to "perform," some totally clueless. On Tuesday nights after 10pm a predominantly gay crowd holds court. —*MH*

SBNY ♂

50 West 17th Street between 5th and 6th Avenues
212-691-0073
Su-Th:4pm-4am; F-Sa: 4pm-5am
Happy Hour: 2 for 1 every night (M-W: 5pm-9pm; Th-Su: 5pm-8pm)
No cover on Monday or Tuesday; W-Su: $5-$15

ALTHOUGH THE NAME (FORMERLY SPLASH) HAS changed and the famous shower (dancers performing under a cascade of water) is gone, the newly renovated and re-christened SBNY remains the quintessential

EROTIC

Tammy Faye Starlite

TOUTED AS THE RAUNCHIEST COUNTRY AND western act this side of the Mason-Dixon line, New York-based performance artist Tammy Lang (known as Tammy Faye Starlite) is the driving force behind her six-piece band, the Angels of Mercy. Tammy's raucous act regularly appears at nightclubs around the city. A little bit country with a big erotic twist, Tammy, embracing her on-stage persona, gyrates and genuflects to songs like "Did I Shave My Vagina for This?" and "God Has Lodged a Tenant in My Uterus." Satirical takes on Christian values, country music, and drug use make for a hilarious act.

Tammy's voice is raspy and high-pitched, but loaded with passion. She resembles a full-faced angel, with long, bright, blonde hair, and her outfits range from country trash to lingerie and leather boots (a la the *Rocky Horror Picture Show*). When she's not with the Angels of Mercy, Miss Tammy fronts the Mike Hunt Band (www.mhuntltd.com/index.html), a Rolling Stones tribute band, of sorts. Playing the role of Mick Jagger opposite Jill Richmond's (from The Aquanettes) Keith Richards, Tammy moves, sings and struts just like the main Stone himself.

At Tammy's website, you can find out when and where she's performing next, as well as keep tabs on her bible studies and progress in rehab. You can also order her first CD, *On My Knees*, soon to be followed by *Used Country Female*. —MU

www.tammyfayestarlite.com

Chelsea boy bar. The accent here is on beef—beefy go-go boys, bartenders, and patrons. All eyes are on the shirtless, but it's a comfortable place to go dancing even if you don't spend six days a week at the gym.

SBNY is all about seeing and being seen—the new floor plan features an elliptical bar that allows patrons to sip drinks while never losing sight of the crowd. It's also the cruisiest place you could hope for, so your chances of going home alone are pretty slim. Go downstairs to check your coat and while you're at it, take a peek in the clean and spacious bathroom, which features video monitors above the urinals. If the club gets you in the mood for some post-dance action, there's a merchandise hut where you can purchase fashionable underwear, swimsuits, and club gear, as well as condoms, lube, and porn videos.

The downstairs bar provides a quiet oasis where you can comfortably chat up the boy you just met on the dance floor above. Video monitors ring the perimeter of the dance floor and alternately show sexy clips of boys working out in Speedos and scenes from kitschy old television shows. There's also a laser show and plenty of backlit mirrors. The go-go boys are pure beef, as are the bartenders (some are so muscle bound, its amazing they can still make change). And the music (courtesy of some talented and guest DJs) is great—a throbbing, pulsating mix of dance tracks that should keep you going all night long. —*JS/MHB*

Stella's

266 West 47th Street between Broadway and 8th Avenue
212-575-1680
Daily: noon-4am
Happy hour: daily, noon-8pm
Cover charge varies

VARIOUS AND SUNDRY SHADY CHARACTERS ROAM the theater district—you'll find a phantom, a lion, and Michael Flatley. But none are as sketchy as the characters who prowl Stella's, home to a seedy spectacle featuring a few beauties, a couple of beasts, and even some average queers. One of the bar's main draws is its production of *Rent*. No, not the show. Stella's interpretation boasts a licentious cast of men in their late 40s and 50s renting younger males to act out various scenes at home.

But relax, not everyone in this watering hole is thirsty to get his hole filled—at least not by having to pay for play.

Since most of the men here will soon enter the Viagra stage of their lives, this is also a great neighborhood bar for boys searching for daddies and vice versa. Thus, if you're a young stud who dreams of taking center stage, Stella's provides an audience craving your attention. And if you're an older gent, you'll find plenty of peers to chat with. Whether you're here to buy a beer or buy a guy, just remember that although theaters surround the bar, drama queens should rehearse their scenes elsewhere.

Touting itself as "New York's World Class Midtown Bar," the small tavern flaunts deluxe attractions such as a pool table, three video games, and $3.25 draft beers during happy hour. To remind you that you're in theaterland, posters from Broadway shows line the dark wooden walls, and show tunes occasionally penetrate the smoky air. And to remind you that you're in a "world class" setting, a plunger is at your disposal in the tiny bathroom, where patrons rarely close stall doors and often keep their eyes and flys open.

If viewing the clientele doesn't entertain you, perhaps Stella's lords of the dance will. Every night at 11:30, dancers thrust and grind to the beat of tunes that show off their packages. On weekends, they also go down—stairs, that is—to a dark, cruisy basement floor. But don't let the darkness scare you—a spotlight will shine on you as long as you're eager to mingle and have fun. —*VL*

Stonewall Inn/ Stonewall Bistro

53 Christopher Street at Sheridan Square
212-463-0950
Daily: 3pm-4am
Happy Hour: M-F: 3pm-9pm, two-for-one drinks
($3 frozen margaritas on Sa-Su, 3pm-9pm)

THIS LEGENDARY BAR HAS A SPECIAL PLACE IN THE history of the gay liberation movement. On June 27, 1969 when neighborhood gays refused to be pushed around any longer by a hostile police force, they responded in what has come to be known as the weeklong Stonewall Rebellion.

Quite a bit has changed over the years at 53 Christopher Street, but what's remained constant is the loyal following that this neighborhood gathering place has engendered. A recent renovation breathed new life into the main bar area and an upstairs dance floor has been a welcome addition. A good deal of the erotic heat at Stonewall is generated by the go-go boys, who perform every night except Wednesdays.

Lots of dark wood and comfortable booth seating opposite the bar on the first floor provide an inviting, clubby feel. A pool table towards the back leads to a smaller, cozy bar area with a staircase leading up to the second floor. The new color scheme (light leather-hued walls with plum accents) carries from the first floor to the spacious dance floor and accompanying bar upstairs. New bathroom facilities on both floors are generously-sized, private, and spotless.

Connected to the bar at 113 Seventh Avenue South is the new Stonewall Bistro (open 7 days, 4:30pm-2am), which carries through Stonewall Inn's elegant new design scheme. More light leather-colored walls, plum ceilings and accents, and plenty of gauzy tan and plum curtains dress up the Bistro's cozy dining room/bar area. A black baby grand piano sits in the front window and its player fills the room with music seven nights a week.

Excellent food and friendly service complete a classy dining experience suitable for a date, special occasion, or a dinner with mom. Dinner entrées range from $9.95 to $22.95 and there's a prix fixe Sunday brunch from 11:30am-3:30pm for $10.95.

P.S.—check out the bathroom. Trust us on this one.

—MJN

The Web

40 East 58th Street between Park and Madison Avenues
212-308-1546
M-F: 4pm-4am; Sa: 8pm-4am; Su: 9pm-4am
Su-W: free; Th: free before 10 pm, $5 after;
F-Sa: $8 before 11pm, $10 after

PAN-ASIAN AND WOMEN-FRIENDLY WITH A RE-
freshing lack of pretense, The Web is the perfect spot
for rice queens and their admirers. Fantastic go-go boys,
mostly, but not exclusively Asian, rotate from stage to cage
to cube throughout the night, usually dancing with at
least their muscular butts exposed (we were particularly
fond of the Sal Mineo look-alike).

The décor has a decidedly Robotech Japanimation vibe,
while Chinese lanterns and disco balls maintain links with
tradition. Two bars located around an upper balcony, a
lower dance floor, and a billiard room/arcade provide
ample space for mixing, mingling, or just
hanging out. Video monitors play queer-Asian fare that
perfectly complement the Cher-heavy Eurotech dance mix.
It's the only Asian gay club in New York (believe it or not)
and is comfortable for Asians looking to meet each other,
Asians looking to meet non-Asians, and non-Asians looking to be met. The crowd is about three-quarters Asian.

Special events include Eurasian night on Wednesdays
featuring Eastern European and Asian go-go boys; Frat
House Thursday with college go-go boys; Funk Fridays
with DJ Mosley and go-go boys all night; and Men's Night
on Saturdays with J. Mo spinning and go-go boys all
night. Check your pants at the door or show your boxers
or briefs on Mondays and get a free drink. —*JS/MHB*

HOT FASHIONS

NEW YORK IS AN UNDISPUTED FASHION CAPITAL, not only for couture, but for erotic garb as well. Whether you're looking for a hot little number in leather, lace, or latex, a full bodysuit in rubber, a maid's or nurse's outfit, or a seductive corset, the shops listed in this section should be able to satisfy your fancy.

What you wear can dramatically alter how you're perceived by those around you, as well as how you perceive yourself. As some say, "you are what you wear." The most introverted plain-Jane, can be magically transformed into a femme fatale simply by stepping into a tightly-laced corset and a pair of spike-heeled boots. Erotic attire can boost self-confidence, make you more gregarious, and break down inhibitions. And it's a lot cheaper than psychotherapy!

If you agree that clothes make the man or woman, then you might also agree that sartorial style is especially important for the man or the woman on the make. What you wear can make an enormous difference not only in whether you get laid, but also in how much you enjoy the pursuit and act of sex.

But for many, just the thought of dressing up in a blatantly sexy manner induces more than a bit of fear. All those societal messages about what's proper and what's not, have lodged indelibly in our heads and dictate our behavior. And that's precisely why dressing provocatively is so hot. It's an exciting (and harmless) way to flaunt social conventions—be daring. And, as we know, breaking the rules can be fun, leading from one thing to another.

Sexy dressing may be tied to some deep, dark fetish or might simply involve the desire to show off a little more bod than usual. But fundamentally, it's all about fantasy. When you put on the right clothes for the occasion, you become transformed, and like an actor in a play you're ready to fully explore an entirely new persona. So before going out (or staying in) for an erotic evening, consider your fantasies. Who do you want to become and why? Does the idea of turning yourself into a tall, slutty blonde in vinyl turn you on? Do you get hard envisioning yourself as a rough and tough leather man? How would you feel in a nurse's uniform? Go with your gut and seek out the costume that will bring you as close to your fantasy as possible.

Leather, latex, silk, rubber, and vinyl are materials of choice for many erotic dressers, but remember, it's your fantasy and you can wear what you like. Wearing latex simply because you've heard that it's supposed to be sexy won't do anything for your libido. Then again, it's a good idea to consider the occasion you're dressing for. For example, going to an S&M club in deck shoes, khakis, and a tennis sweater probably won't get you much action.

If you're a little nervous about what's going to fit and look hot, take a friend or lover with you when you shop, especially if it's the first time around. Considering how difficult certain clothing is to put on, you'll probably need an extra hand anyway. The shopping experience alone can be a huge turn-on and you might just get the chance to experience the pleasures of dressing-room sex. —*TH/MU*

The Baroness

212-529-5964
By appointment only
www.baroness.com

IF YOU'RE NEITHER A FETISHIST NOR A MATERIALS
freak, you have no compelling reason to ponder the wondrous nature of latex. It's a natural—and expensive—
product (derived from the sap of the rubber tree), that
comfortably holds and molds the body, feels sexy to wear
and touch, and even smells yummy—like a chocolaty
malt sundae. But visit The Baroness, New York's premier
designer of elegant latex fashions, at her atelier in
Alphabet City, and not only will you learn about the fascinating properties of latex, you stand a strong chance of
being seduced by its sensual qualities.

Flame-haired proprietress, The Baroness, who officially
changed her name eleven years ago to this regal, evocative
moniker, approaches latex with the fervor borne of a
decade-long obsession. Others may want to buy the world
a coke, but The Baroness prefers to swath it in latex—
preferably hers. Latex is her medium, but it's also a
metaphor for her life philosophy—forgiving and flattering
in its all-direction pliability, sensual in its pool-like luster,
luxurious, glamorous, and distinctly appealing. The
Baroness, a former costume and lingerie designer, is a latex
pioneer, having taken the material from its most common
form—super-tight black or red garb worn exclusively
behind closed doors—into previously unexplored stratos-
pheres of usage, color, and fit. A good example would be her
magnificent, sweeping cape in the pale yellow translucency
of the substance in its undyed state. And the experimenta-
tion has paid off: The Baroness' website gets upwards of
60,000 hits a day, and her fashions have been featured in
many publications from *The Village Voice* to *Interview*.

The Baroness offers three lines. Elegant, Provocative
Fashions, priced from $50 to $800, features simply cut
men's and women's garments available in a vivid Crayola
rainbow of colors, such as the electric blue, high-necked,

long-sleeved "governess dress" Kim Basinger wore on a late 1990s cover of Detour. The Baroness doesn't believe latex will ever be mainstream, but this line offers the sexy, lubricious designs any body-conscious urban warrior might choose for an evening out.

The two newest lines, Bizarre Rubber Contraptions ($600 and up) and Fit For Royalty (totally outrageous made-to-order garments, priced accordingly), are strictly for fetishists: the Contraptions line includes items such as hooded body bags and inflatable straitjackets; Royalty offers Renaissance-style ball gowns; mermaid outfits, complete with functional, removable tail; and other fetishistic party-going ensembles.

In her boutique, The Baroness creates a one-on-one environment where she can win over a stylish novice or protect the anonymity of a private cross-dresser. Her workmanship is painstaking and guaranteed for a lifetime. Call for an appointment, visit the website (www.baroness.com), or look for The Baroness label in specialty boutiques around town.

Once a month, The Baroness hosts a Fetish Retinue at the Alphabet Lounge (Avenue C at 7th Street), billed as "extreme dress and play in an intimate environment." —JAT

Bodyhints
462 West Broadway between Houston and Prince Streets
212-777-8677
M-Th: 11am-7pm; F-Sa: 11am-8pm; Su: noon-6pm
www.bodyhints.com

♀

THIS SHOP FOR ELEGANT, SEXY INTIMATE APPAREL was founded by husband-and-wife team Allen and Lauren Blankenship—formerly senior vice presidents at Playboy—who opened their 2,000-square-foot emporium in October 2001. Couples, single women, and in-the-know men browse around the bright, loft-like main floor before heading downstairs to the sales area ("bargain basement" doesn't do justice to the reduced-priced samples). Unlike the merchandise displays at itty-bitty boutiques (where items are typically crammed into disorganized drawers that only store employees can access), all the pretty undies at Bodyhints hang or are stacked neatly Gap-style out in the open, which means shoppers never have to hunt for a salesperson. Not that they'd have trouble finding sartorial assistance. Service is overwhelmingly friendly and helpful, with knowledgeable staff at the ready to retrieve whatever-sized item—from 32A to 40F—a customer may need.

The Blankenships hit Paris at least twice a year to load up on their favorite French, Italian, and Brazilian brands rarely found on this side of the pond: Lise Charmel features colorful embroidery and appliqués that aren't itchy or elaborate, while Bracli's "pearl thong" ($20) continues to be a top seller. With stretchy nude fabric pieces held together by clear, super-strong plastic hip and crotch straps, the "world's smallest" G-string from Aubade ($20) is likely the globe's least noticeable, too. Saucy girls nostalgic for childhood will love Cherry Pie's cotton panties embroidered with a trio of dollar signs ($17.75) or days of the week ($69 for a set of Sunday through Saturday panties). Bodyhints also sells seamless basics from Hanro, the label lining many an uptown girl's lingerie drawer, as well as an in-store line of robes and panties. One display area is devoted entirely to basics in black, nude, and white. After playing dress-up (or is that undress-up?) in the luxurious fitting rooms, be sure to check out the small but choice selection of Cabana Club robes, Davies Gate luxe votives, and Get Fresh body care products. —*EH*

I used to be Snow White—
but I drifted.

—Mae West

EROTIC

Changes

581 9th Avenue, Suite 3B
between 41st and 42nd Streets
646-473-0184
M, T, Th, F: 2-8pm; W: 12-6pm; Sa: 12:30-7:30pm
www.changestvboutique.com
www.morphe.bigstep.com

WHEN LEE'S MARDI GRAS, AN APPAREL AND AC-
cessories purveyor, closed its doors in 1999, the transgender community went into mourning. But just two years
later, Leslie—an active participant in the transgender scene
for over two decades—has filled the gap with Changes.

At this cheery shop, transvestite (TV) veterans and
newbies alike will find a variety of garb (sizes range from
men's small to 4X) and shoes (up to size 17) to choose
from. Silicone falsies sell for two-thirds the market rate,
including full breasts ($136 for triangle-shaped boobs,
$168 for teardrop-shaped ones) and push-up inserts
($35). The satin (from $5) and crotchless lace ($12)
panties are well priced, too. Whether for bedroom play,
club hopping, or daily wear, flattening that manly bulge
with a gaff—a buttless sheath designed to hold the male
member down ($15)—makes it easier to slip into a lace
body stocking or mesh bodysuit (from $15).

The boutique also carries fancy frocks picked up on
consignment from the trannie extravaganza Night of
1,000 Gowns and PVC mini skirts with naughty, corset-
style lacing. But the shoes, terrifically affordable, are
arguably the best reason to shop here. Practical folks will
want to stock up on basic leather pumps ($30), while shoe
fetishists will dig the more frivolous offerings, such as
feathered mules in turquoise ($40), hot pink sequined
pumps ($45), and mirror-bedecked, Lucite platforms with
blinking lights ($75). The total TV look would not be
complete without a costume-quality fall or wig, or
Dermablend cover-up cream (to hide those blemishes and
in-grown beard hairs). And for those who are especially

serious about their appearance, Leslie can arrange for private cosmetics lessons with a makeup artist.

If you're more interested in monitoring the scene than participating in it, check out such periodicals as *Transvestite Times*, *LadyLike*, and *Transvestite Tapestry*.   —EH

DeMask

135 West 22nd Street between 6th & 7th Avenues
212-352-2850
M-W, F: 11a.m.-7pm; Th: 12pm-8pm; Sa: 12pm-7pm; Su: 12pm-6pm
www.demask.com

LEAVE IT TO AMSTERDAM, THAT WIDE OPEN CITY, to bring S&M paraphernalia and fetish fashion out of the closet and into the mainstream. Originally an English rubber and leather apparel manufacturer, DeMask opened its first retail shop in The Netherlands in 1989. The New York location—the only one in the U.S.—opened in 1998. The company is planning to open six more stores around the world within the next five years. Perhaps a decade from now Demask will sit side by side with the Gap and Banana Republic at malls nationwide.

DeMask is situated on a quiet side street in Chelsea, but there's nothing subtle about the latex-clad mannequins which grace its shop windows. Inside, moody track lighting illuminates purple and black fixtures and the unmistakable smell of rubber tickles your nostrils. Ambient music further enhances the sexy vibe. And if you like what you hear, you're probably in luck, as DeMask carries on CD much of the background music it plays.

The shop's main floor is devoted primarily to apparel and footwear, including latex dresses and skirts, catsuits, masks, and halter tops. As you'll quickly realize, fetish clothing here does not come cheap—latex dresses will run you around $175 and catsuits can gouge your wallet for as much as $400.

To view the hardcore stuff, take the metal stairs down to the basement. But be forewarned: this is no place for

the uninitiated—DeMask doesn't carry Pocket Rockets or other mainstream sex toys. Instead, display cases present S&M accoutrements like paddles, enema bags, gynecological tools, inflatable butt plugs, ball weights, nipple clamps, and even an electro-shock kit.

Thankfully, the sales help is rather unobtrusive. You can browse undisturbed for hours in your own private Marquis de Sade fantasy, but rest assured, if you ask for assistance these folks are happy to provide it, and are quite knowledgeable about their products.

"We believe that fetish clothing is really for the new millennium," says the store's manager. He says the store attracts customers from across the board—from bankers to prostitutes "to Chinese grandmas looking for a raincoat." After all, rubber is water repellent. —*JG*

Gaelyn & Cianfarani
155 East 2nd Street between Avenues A and B
212-614-6998
W-Su: 1pm-8pm
www.latexdesigner.com

FROM COUTURE DRESSES THAT ACCENTUATE TITS and ass, to codpiece-enhanced briefs that protect your package, this clothing boutique knows what the hot body wants. The designers/owners, Genevieve and Atom, are purveyors of fine latex and rubber fashion. Their expertise with the material, along with their classic tailoring skills makes you want to keep the rubber on, even during sex.

The clean shop/studio displays their styles in a variety of colors and sizes. Of course there are the black catsuits, corsets, and chaps, but imagine wearing the latex pencil skirt to work, the latex cocktail dress to a party, or the supermanesque padded latex shirt to the gym (though not to work out in). Dresses, tops, and bottoms (some with less bottom than others) share space with men's briefs, cowboy shirts, biker pants, and haute S&M-inspired

accessories and jewelry. A customer favorite is the Flamenco dress that's easy on and easy off, thanks to a two-way zipper. Strategic cutouts, lacing, and multi-paneled construction make the experience of dressing in G & C latex like being in a body-stiletto. Items can be tailor-made, but some are available off the rack in small, medium, and large. And if the available designs (inspired by everything from 1930s undergarments to Alexander McQueen) don't make you pant, G & C will work with you to create one that will.

Dresses range from $288 for the Cocktail to $838 for the Flamenco. Separates vary widely from $58 for briefs to $868 for biker pants made of recycled bicycle inner tubes (cleaned, conditioned, and meticulously sewn). Accessories are a good starter at $10 for rubber wrist cuffs, to $88 for Xena-worthy gauntlets. Whatever your shape or desire, all you need is a generous major credit card.

Tarty vegans, urban cowboys, and prim dominatrixes rejoice! —LL

Gothic Renaissance

108 4th Avenue between 11th and 12th Streets
212-780-9554
M-Sa: 11am-8pm; Su: noon-7pm

Halloween Adventure

104 4th Avenue between 11th and 12th Streets
212-673-4546
M-Sa: 11am-8pm, Su: noon-7pm
www.halloweenadventure.com

A COSTUME SHOP WITH FANGS, GOTHIC RENaissance caters mainly to the Vampyre and Goth-Industrial crowd. There are lots of velvet capes and goblets, Victorian and Renaissance-style shirts for men, clothing by the goth labels Lip Service and Shrine. They

Body Modification

HOMO SAPIENS IS THE ONLY SPECIES THAT INtentionally modifies its appearance. For thousands of years in primitive societies, man has used his flesh as a canvas to express such concepts as status, wealth, power, and tribal membership. In contemporary society, we change our bodies mostly out of a need for self-expression or self-improvement. The purpose of a piercing or tattoo, a nose job or breast enlargement is primarily to enhance our sexual allure.

So are piercings and tattoos inherently erotic? We think not, especially since they have become so commonplace, but some can be extremely sexy—particularly if placed near, on, or through the body's primary erogenous zones; or feature some sort of erotic imagery. A tattoo that accentuates the curve of a woman's back can be extremely hot, and although we can't say from personal experience, we're told that piercings of the nipples, the hood of the clitoris, and certain parts of the penis can result in vastly enhanced sexual stimulation.

Given that there are umpteen thousand shops in the Big Apple where you can get a tattoo or piercing, we've decided to list only a few of the best. Whether you visit these or other establishments, give some serious thought be-

fore offering up your flesh. Here are a few words of caution:

If you plan on getting a piercing, make sure that the studio you select subscribes to the highest standards of hygiene. Single-use needles, autoclave sterilization, ultrasonic cleaners, and cold sterile solutions for items that can't take the heat are all a must. Cheap jewelry can increase the risk of infection, so stick with high quality ornaments made of surgical stainless steel, 14- or 18-karat solid gold, niobium, or titanium. Before leaving the studio, you should be thoroughly informed about proper aftercare for your piercing, and encouraged to follow up if you have piercing-related questions during the weeks ahead.

If you're in the market for a tattoo, pick a studio that looks clean and boasts new equipment in good working order. Ask to see several photos of your prospective artist's work before getting in the chair. Look carefully at where the lines in any design come to a point—the lines should be straight and the point should be sharp. Unfortunately, it takes about six months before you can tell how your tattoo is going to look over the long haul. If, after six months, the lines of the image begin to appear uneven, then you know that the original needlework was sub par. —*TH*

ANIL GUPKA AT INKLINE STUDIO [513 E. 5th St #1A between Avenues A and B; 212-614-0094; Tu-Sa: 3pm-11pm]

What appears from the outside to be your run-of-the-mill East Village apartment is the workplace of Anil Gupta, one of the most renowned tattoo artists in the city. Gupta's creations have been featured on The Discovery Channel and Ripley's Believe It or Not, and his clients come from all corners of the globe. Photos of his tattoo artistry—including uncanny lifelike portraits of Frank Sinatra and Jimi Hendrix—line the studio's walls. Though Gupta's schedule is nearly always booked three months in advance, the wait for an initial consultation ($50) is generally only a few days. During the appointment, you can discuss with Anil the look you want to achieve, and he will let you know when the work can be done and how much it will cost. Anil is a serious artist—so cover-ups, tribal work, or basic lettering are not among the services he offers. —*MJ*

DRAGON FLY'S ELECTRIC TATTOO GALLERY [158 W. 15th St. between 6th and 7th Avenues; 212-255-1490; Daily: noon- ▶

7pm; www.dragonflytattoo.com)

Dragon Fly—a trained painter, graduate of the School of Visual Arts, and longtime associate of the renowned Spider Webb—bought this business from Spider in 2001. Along with Andria and Spider, she specializes in customized tattoos, though patrons are welcome to look through the flash books and portfolios in the waiting area for inspiration. Virtually any style is handled here, including traditional, tribal (solid black), fantasy, abstract, graffiti, and sexy. Rates for tattoos depend on the time required to complete a piece. Appointments are encouraged, but if you're feeling spontaneous, walk-ins are also accepted. An adjacent gallery space showcasing painting and photography is open to the public by appointment. —PG

GOTHAM (211 West 20th Street between 7th and 8th Avenues; 212-229-0180; Tu-W: noon-8pm; Th-Sa: noon-10pm; Su: noon-5pm; www.gothamworld.com)

This dark, basement-level piercing parlor attracts an eclectic clientele ranging from modern punks with pink Mohawks to J. Crew model types. Gotham's roots lie in San Francisco where its owners once worked for the revered Gauntlet before casting out on their own. An autoclave is used to disinfect all tools and jewelry. Piercings run between $30 for a simple navel or ear to $45 for more complex work. Jewelry ranges from $20 to $1000. —KG

SACRED BODY ART EMPORIUM (365 Canal Street. bet West Broadway & Wooster Street; 212-226-4286; M-Sa: 9am-9pm; Su: 11am-6pm; www.sacredtattoo.com)

In business for more than a decade, Sacred boasts a clientele that includes Howard Stern, Casey Affleck, and Summer Phoenix. You can get inked by one of nine tattoo artists (rates are $100/hour with a $50 minimum). Kanji—Chinese characters imported to Japan in the 5th century via Korea—is the tattoo design of choice here. If piercing is your pleasure ($80 for a genital piercing, $30 for a nipple piercing), you'll have lots of options in that department as well. Sacred maintains the highest standards of hygiene and all its artists are independently licensed and certified by the Board of Health. —GM can outfit you as a Renaissance bride, a nun from hell, or with red or purple butterfly wings by Lisa Lost for a faerie ball. If masquerade balls are your thing, don't miss the Mardi Gras masques imported from Venetian designer, Si Lucia, which range from simple velvet animal-prints to baroque gold and roses.

While the atmosphere at Gothic Renaissance is more Tim Burton than The Baroness, the budding domina will find a nice selection of corsets in a variety of materials—leather-look, vinyl, and brocade—all black, naturally. Next to the over-the-top pieces by self-proclaimed "Metallic Messiah" jeweler Axel were some chain-mail bracelets and neckpieces for sale on consignment.

Two doors down is Halloween Adventure, where you can complete your outfit from their huge inventory of costume accessories. They stock fake chastity belts for men and women, whips and rubber chest plates, and other fun fetish gear. They carry makeup by Ben Nye, Kryolan, Backstage, and Woochie, custom fangs, hats, and an enormous selection of wigs. Play out your fantasy—Marie Antoinette, British barrister, Dutch girl, Keith Partridge shag, and for the budding Monica Lewinskys among us, the thick, graying mane of "Mr. President."

Sorry folks, but there are no rentals. —*EL*

Hotel Venus

382 West Broadway between Spring and Broome Streets
212-966-4066
Daily: 11am–8pm
www.patriciafield.com

PATRICIA FIELD, CLOTHES STYLIST FOR *SEX AND THE City*, opened this enormous Pandora's box of a shop just a few years ago. Mostly clothing, the store, at first glance, resembles a tizzy Halloween parade, but unfolds to reveal itself as a makeup and hair salon, wig museum, publishing house, erotic gift shop…you could get lost in it for hours. The staff boasts that Britney Spears and Tommy Lee are just a couple of the celebs who have been known to cruise the racks. Much of the fashion is '80s trash disco (was there any other kind?) morphed with cutesy Japanese cyberpunk coupled with queer goth. We tried on a Marine's hat that would work well at any military fuck club. There's pretty much anything you need if you're dressing for maximum party effect. The store caters to the larger-sized cross-dressing customer, offering ladies shoes up to size 13, and short dresses for the taller girls. We've heard that there is a worrying trend these days away from the feather boa and towards the preppy, but happily, this store rights the wrong.

Interesting items from smaller labels range from styled punk to party fetish to street (summer) wear. And for those who don't mind being screwed by the established fashion houses, there are Gucci and Louis Vuitton cock rings. Other popular items include T-shirts emblazoned with monstrous porn star erections, a selection of smutty underwear (men's and women's), nipple enhancers and tassels, fetishwear, PVC, and good ol' bondagewear.

The wigs are wondrous. Cute Joey, who also works the makeup booth, mostly makes them in house or on request. In a trice, he can transform you into a Hedwig wannabe, a cum-hither geisha, or even a lascivious Carol Brady. Prices start at around $125.

The staff is enthused and interesting. One edits the store magazine (on sale for $6), another DJs some of the bigger dance parties, and another just sells himself well. Don't forget to buy! —*TM*

Ian's New York City

5 St. Mark's Place between 2nd and 3rd Avenues
212-420-1857
M-Sa: noon-8pm; Su: 1pm-7pm

1151 2nd Avenue between 60th and 61st Streets
212-838-3969
M-Sa: 11am-7pm; Su: call (hours vary by season)

TUCKED BENEATH MUNCHY'S DELI AND ADJACENT
to the eye-catching Religious Sex, Ian's downtown location is easy to miss when strolling St. Mark's Place, but
don't pass it by. The small, but well-stocked, subterranean
store is worth a closer look as it offers a quality array of
playwear, streetwear, and gothwear.

Vinyl-like PVC and velvet abound. A bestseller and
personal favorite is the Nurse Mini ($56), which "covers
just enough," as co-owner Lou Valentine pointed out.
This low-cut white PVC zip-up mini-dress (available in
small, medium, large) is decorated with a red cross over
the breast and comes with a matching hat to complete
the Florence Nightingale look. As any good nurse
knows, appropriate footwear is key. Fortunately, Ian's
offers a nice variety of stilettos ($55 and up) and patent
leather spikes by Dallas Heights ($70)—perfect for the
head nurse on duty.

Looking for something medieval? Try one of the myr-
iad Goth gowns or cat suits ($65 and up). Again, you
won't have to go far to find footwear. Pick from platforms
($60 and up), knee-high boots ($65 and up) and—when
in stock—thigh-highs ($175 and up). The latter are a hot
item and tend to go fast, so it's best to check in periodi-
cally if you're interest is high-button shoes.

Still feel like something's missing? Accessorize with
items from behind the counter such as tights and stockings, fetish masks, and jewelry—including the impaling
kind. Ian's offers comprehensive in-house body piercing,
from the popular tongue and navel to the more stimulating genital and nipple punctures. All dressed up and no

place to go? Pick up one of the many flyers for assorted naughty club nights on your way out.

At Ian's uptown location you'll find fewer studs and more rhinestones. The store is swank and well lit with Elvis crooning on the airwaves to complete the mood. Uptown mainly carries dancewear for the stripper sophisticate and Hefneresque suits for the gentlemen. You'll find lots of silky dresses and tight halters as well as some of the same playwear from downtown and a wealth of stilettos. The baby blue chenille tube dress by Ilysse Foster was irresistible—especially when Ian himself offered to knock 50% off the price tag! (It was bound for the sale rack so he cut me an early bird special. What a doll.)

Both locations have been long in service, 18 years downtown and 25 years uptown. Between the two of them, it shouldn't be hard to find some kicks. —*SC*

La Petite Coquette

51 University Place between 9th and 10th Streets
212-473-2478
M-W: 11am-7pm; Th: 11am-8pm; F-Sa: 11am-7pm;
Su: noon-6pm
www.lapetitecoquette.com   ♀

FOR FINE, EUROPEAN-STYLE LINGERIE, LOOK NO further than La Petite Coquette, which, by the way, translates as "the little flirt." Since 1978, this adorable, bi-level Greenwich Village shop, has been wowing its loyal clientele with an incredible array of high-end thongs, bras, robes slips, corsets, boy shorts, and more. The shop's owner, Rebecca Aspan—dubbed by the press as the "guru" of lingerie—asserts that her selection is second to none and we would have to agree. The clientele, by the way, isn't too shabby either. Happy customers include such notable celebrities as Liza Minelli, Britney Spears, Liv Tyler, and Naomi Campbell. The shop has also been prominently mentioned on Sex in the City.

Much of the merchandise—which comes in a broad range of colors and delectable fabrics—is neatly tucked away in elegant drawers. A "display" board exhibiting the essentials is provided for convenience, but if you don't see what you're looking for just ask. The amiable and knowledge-able sales staff is more than happy to be of assistance. We were told that on more than one occasion a salesperson has received a "kiss" for helping a bewildered customer make the right purchase. One woman, who has been shopping at La Petite Coquette for six years, confided in us that she is so comfortable in the store that she considers it to be an extension of her lingerie chest.

On the "erotic meter" the two items that scored the highest were the "Peek-a-boo-in-the-back" silk panty from England ($150) and the "broccoli" lingerie from Spain, which contrary to popular belief is not a cruciferous veg-etable. If you have money to burn, consider the crystal bra and thong which goes for $1100 —*FM/CL*

Le Corset

80 Thompson Street between Spring and Broome Streets
212-334-4936
Daily: 11am-7pm
www.selimaoptique.com

♀

JUST A GLANCE AT LE CORSET'S WINDOW DISPLAY tells you that this is a shop for serious lingerie fanatics. Although you won't find anything here that can be cate-gorized as kinky, you will find some of the most elegant and sexy lingerie in the city. For men, however, the pick-ings are slim. The only option for guys (except for guys who like to wear women's lingerie), are the silk boxers ($32), which sit right by the shop's entrance. The rest of the merchandise is strictly for the lady of the house.

Feeling a bit weary from our walk downtown, we were immediately attracted to the sleepwear section, which includes pajamas made of a variety of fabrics including wool, silk, and lace. Prices range from $75 to $470. Bras ($70), panties ($30), and thongs ($20) are more of a bargain, and come in a huge selection of fabrics and colors. Without a doubt, however, the highlight here is the collection of corsets ($210) that come in every imaginable color. You'll spend hours trying them on, and deciding which one flatters your waist the most. But before undressing, you might want to take a gander at who is lurking outside your fitting room, as the curtains are see-through. Ooh la la! Also worth a closer look are the reasonably priced garter belts. You can skip the downstairs section altogether, which offers rather expensive ($125) and unattractive bathing suits and negligees ($270). —*FM/CL*

I Love a Man (or Woman) in Uniform

THERE'S SOMETHING PERVERSELY SEXY ABOUT uniforms. Perhaps it's the sense of control and power that they imply; or in some cases (e.g., maids and butlers) it might be that the opposite impression is conveyed—one of subservience. Whatever the reason, they certainly are a lot of fun to put on and take off. Here are three shops where you can indulge your fetish for uniforms:

B & R UNIFORMS CENTER [246 East 23rd Street near 2nd Avenue; 212-679-7674; M-Sa: 10am-6pm]

Close to hospital row, this bright, clean shop offers some excellent deals, particularly for those who like to play doctor and nurse. Colorful scrub tops and bottoms in sizes XS-XL are a steal at $9.99. Add a real stethoscope for just $19.99 to complete the look. B & R also has a selection of vests in black and red [$24.99] for both butlers and maids. The full maid's outfit in black with white trim [$46.99] was especially sexy. There are three dressing rooms so there's virtually no wait for trying on clothes.

DORNAN UNIFORMS [84-18 Astoria Boulevard, Queens, NY;

The Leatherman

111 Christopher Street between Bleecker
and Hudson Streets
212-243-5339
M-Sa: noon-10pm; Su: noon-8pm
www.theleatherman.com

THE LEATHERMAN, FOUNDED BY OWNER CHUCK
Mueller, opened its doors at this prime Christopher Street
location in 1965—way back when the street was still a
ghetto. Rob, the cute, knowledgeable sales associate, let on
that the Leatherman's leather pants, the best of which run
around $375, have definitely hugged the asses of some A-
list celebrities, but he would only mention Lou Reed and

212-247-0937; M-F: 8:30am-4:30pm, Saturdays by appointment; gpiro@dormanuniforms.com)

If you've ever fantasized about having an affair with a doorman at a posh, Park Avenue high-rise; or, if you've ever dreamed
about being a doorman and giving a little extra special service to
some of your residents, a purchase from Dornan Uniforms might
just be the ticket to ecstasy for yourself or that special someone.
Dornan carries an extensive selection of high-quality doorman
duds in a wide range of sizes and colors. No rentals are offered,
but they do provide a cleaning service.

O.K. UNIFORM (368 Broadway between Franklin & White
Streets; 212-791-9789; M-Th: 9:30am-5:30pm; F: 9:30am-
1:30pm; Sa: closed; Su: 11:30am-3:30pm)

This venerable New York institution—whose clients include
Law & Order, *The Cosby Show*, and the Metropolitan Opera—sells
uniforms for a variety of service industries including medical,
hotel, and security. From footwear to scrub caps, gloves to
aprons, it's all here. A complete line of formal wear and tuxedos
for men is also in stock. The staff is extremely helpful, but it's
best not to let on why you're shopping there. They don't really
need to know about your personal fetishes! There are no rentals
here and the return policy is stringent (there is a restocking fee),
so consider your purchase to be final. —*MU/TH*

Andy Warhol by name. Rob added that the store is "adult with a capital A, not adult as in dirty."

The leather aficionado will have plenty to feast his or her eyes on here, including harnesses ($60-$200)—with an entire line for dildo-wearing women; hats—baseball, trooper, biker, and more ($35-$100); bullwhips ($65-$135); riding crops $39.95; canes ($25.95); and slings ($149.25 for a portable sling with padding; $399.50 for a deluxe, heavy duty sling with pillow and stirrups). Of the non-leather items, we were partial to the "cum rag" ($11) and the coded, colored handkerchiefs ($3.50 each). A light blue in the left pocket, for example, means the wearer wants head, whereas light blue in the right pocket means the wearer is an expert cocksucker.

The clientele is first and foremost gay men, followed by lesbians, S/M enthusiasts, leather fans, and finally tourists. Many of the repeat customers take pride in supporting a gay-owned business and often return to purchase items and accessories such as condoms, lube, toys, cock rings, and the like. Loyal customers like the fact that the store's owner regularly donates items or gift certificates to the annual Leather Pride Night auction and other similar events, and gives a 10% discount to members of GMSMA (Gay Male S/M Activists), Lesbian Sex Mafia, the Eulenspiegel Society, and professional dominatrixes. —SES

London Fetish
84 Christopher Street at 7th Avenue South
212-647-9195
M-Th, Su: 11am-11pm; F-Sa: 11am-1am

THIS BELOW-STREET-LEVEL, FETISH BOUTIQUE IS one classy joint. You'll find an abundance of Catherine Courtney's reasonably priced, beautiful, sexy, and fabulous designs for women in leather, PVC, nylon, and latex. A sampling of Courtney's wares includes a red and black latex bustier ($84.99), a leopard print corset with match-

ing panties ($74.99), a purple latex miniskirt with either lace-up straps, buckles, or zippers ($84.99), and a black nylon full-length bodysuit ($87.99).

The corsets ($110-$350) in pony leather and patent leather are truly amazing. Dominatrix-like PVC trench coats ($420) in red, black, and assorted animal prints will make you look as though you're hosting *The Weakest Link*. And women's vinyl pants come in sky blue, sparkling burgundy, New York black, glistening purple, and shiny silver.

Men have some good options too, including stylish leather pants ($280-$350)—some with leather laces at the ankles; others with a blue, yellow, or red stripe down the leg; or there's always tried and true solid black or brown. If you want to show your support for New York's Finest, check out the black leather short-sleeve shirt with NYPD logo ($269.99).

London also carries S/M merchandise: paddles, whips, floggers, cuffs and the like. Tie-Ups, billed as "the user friendly restraints" can be purchased individually (neck collar—$31.99; wrist and ankle restraints—$27.99; thigh cuffs—$39.99)—or as a set ($59.99 for 9-pieces). You'll also find racks ($99-$150), slings ($225-$500), hoods ($300), masks ($30-$400), and half- and full-body harnesses ($45-$450). Our favorite item, though, was a leather, nail-studded mask ($260). Oh, and lest we forget, London also has body jewelry. —*SES*

Patricia Field
382 W. Broadway between Spring and Broome Streets (at Hotel Venus)
212-254-1699
Daily: 11am-8pm
www.patriciafield.com

THE MALLIFICATION OF MANHATTAN BE DAMNED. Patricia Field continues to offer up impossibly fun, impractical, slightly lascivious fashion for the club-kid and trannie set. Strut along the leopard-print carpet and pluck a tangerine-hued, Tibetan alpaca coat ($800) from the hot-pink walls—a perfect cover-up for that turquoise chain-mail "gown" ($900). Or pair a feather-covered bustier ($250) with a skirt comprised of business card-size, laminated pictures of lips ($180). Not interested in spending $60 plus for a shredded vintage T-shirt? Racks at the back of the first level are always filled with discounted clothes, though most of the sale items are for men. (It's about time a hip shop gave the guys a fashion break!)

Peruse the panty section—a small alcove where comfy elastin-viscose blend thongs, bikinis, and briefs by Cosabella ($16-$38) are the order of the day. For fall 2001, Field joined forces with designer David Dalrymple to launch a long awaited in-store label. Featured are stretchy, body-hugging jumpsuits and shirts with denim detail, plus ruffled lace panties ($36) and matching tube tops ($58) and bandeaus ($30) in head-turning colors like cotton candy pink and lime green. Other white-hot items include garb and accessories seen on *Sex and the City*, for which Field serves as costume designer: Mia & Lizzie gold and diamond horseshoe-pendant necklace ($400-$2,135); Heatherette personalized tee ($125 for up to seven sparkly, silk-screened letters); and Bodyperks fake nipples ($21).

The second-floor, full-service salon goes beyond haircuts (from $75) and extensions (from $600), selling quality costume ($25-$100) and professional-grade ($100-$175) wigs. Stylists of indeterminate gender can trim or set the hairpiece in just about any desired coif (from $30). Those looking for a little House of Field magic, but who don't want to go home with latex hot pants can always head to the front makeup counter for a makeover ($65), lash application ($15), or eyebrow taming ($20).   —*EH*

Religious Sex

7 St. Mark's Place between 2nd and 3rd Avenues
212-477-9037
M-W: noon-8pm; Th-Sa: noon-9pm; Su: 1pm-8pm
www.religioussex.com

KEEP AN EYE OUT FOR ITS TATTERED AWNING BEcause this gothic emporium is easily missed as you fight the tourists crowding the sidewalks of St Mark's Place. Duck inside and you'll find yourself surrounded by racks of clothing in soothing tones of burgundy, black, and forest green. Religious Sex may be small but it's well-stocked with a mishmash of fetish wear suitable for just about anyone—from followers of the Vampire Lestat to Renaissance Faire types. You may even get to shop elbow to elbow with a top stylist as he picks out a few items for a celebrity that he will probably refuse to name.

Whatever your budget, you are likely to find something in the store to your liking. Tights, stockings, studded belts, and novelty underwear are available in a wide range of styles and prices. A pair of black patent leather mules with ostrich feather fluff a la Jean Harlow ($49) contrast nicely with a red patent leather motorcycle jacket with bondage rings by Lip Service ($88). A lush brocade merry widow by Shirley of Hollywood ($98) hangs next to a lavish lace-up gown by Black Kindergarten ($175). Religious Sex carries an extensive collection of hip everyday clothing as well, so you might consider stopping in for a new shirt and toss in a studded collar just for the hell of it.   —LT

Tino of New York

155 8th Avenue at 18th Street, 2nd Floor
212-255-7334 (phone and fax)
M-F: noon-8pm; Sa: noon-9pm; Sunday by appointment
www.tinoleathers.com

EROTIC

"CUTTING EDGE LEATHERS" PROMISES TINO'S black and gold business card, and, mounting the stairs to the small, but well-equipped Chelsea shop, we can attest that it is no lie. The smell of leather alone will warm the cockles of any leather-lover's heart. Just about everything in the shop is made of leather, including the roses in a vase

Miss Vera's Finishing School for Boys Who Want to be Girls

VERONICA VERA—WHOSE REPRESSED, CATHOLIC girlhood propelled her first into a career as a porn star (she's been out of the biz for years) then writer—is a local hero of sorts. She's taken countless transgendered men (mostly well-to-do heterosexuals), and transformed them into beautiful, confident ladies courtesy of Miss Vera's Finishing School for Boys Who Want to Be Girls. The school has twelve deans of specialties ranging from cosmetology to high heels, and offers onsite and distance-learning classes, the latter being ideal for the timid or those living outside the city.

Miss Vera claims to have founded her school out of necessity. While writing a book, she was introduced to a male client who was interested in the art of being a woman. She subsequently advertised her "transformational" consulting services in the newspaper and when the phone began ringing off the hook decided to open the school. The school was not meant to be a parody, but rather was created to help men fulfill their transgender fantasies.

Miss Vera clearly loves what she does and has fond recollections of a number of students including Helen, whom she's never met but has corresponded with by mail. Through Miss Vera's tutelage, Helen has become more open with her own wife and claims to now be more content and accepting of herself. In fact, she has actually gone shopping for a new purse.

Seeing a shift in how transgendered individuals are perceived by outsiders, Miss Vera notes that it's now "easier to take students out and about. Now people come with their entire wardrobes instead of that one hidden outfit. Now a trannie can get all sorts of clothing, have an amazing social life, and be part of an aboveground movement."

Although Miss Vera has received franchise requests, she doesn't currently have plans to open more schools, but would like to bring teachers to different cities and make the school's website more interactive. And she's recently completed a new book, *Cross Dress for Success*, which no doubt will be on the shelves in the near future. She's also interested in offering a class on glamour for women (real women). —CV

212-242-6449   www.missvera.com

by the door.

Geared towards the leather-sex scene, there is fetish, bondage, and sexual paraphernalia on display in the cases and on the racks, but the real cutting-edge action is going on in the workroom at the front of the store. This is where Tino creates his custom designs, which are the mainstay of his work. At one time these creations were available by special order only, but now Tino has opened his doors to the public, so that everyone, from the most demanding connoisseur of the bondage/leather/fetish lifestyle to the curious novice, can come and browse. Or browse and come, as the case may be.

The variety of leather gear is impressive. Items range from leather pants, chaps, BMX-style quilted and padded pants, jodhpurs, shirts, and arm bands to restraints, harnesses, masks, hoods, and sleep bags. And it all comes with Tino's personalized touch—all leatherwork is done on the premises by Tino himself. He finds and selects the finest leathers, which he will only use subject to the customer's approval. He will create a leather piece to your specifications, or else you can flip through the albums of his designs or the racks of ready-to-wear items for inspiration. He works in suede as well as leather, and will customize your favorite denim with leather detailing.

What's a bigger turn-on than a man in a uniform? Why, a man in one of Tino's all-leather police uniforms, one of the shop's most popular items. Complete with authentic police-department patches from the city of your choice, your outfit may be topped off with any of Tino's full range of accessories—from cop-gear to cock rings and dildos. And lest women feel left out, we spied all-leather catsuits and bondagewear that Tino designs just for them.

As if that weren't enough, Tino and his most accommodating staff, offer body piercing as a courtesy to their customers. Tino also does alterations and repair of his pieces, as well as leatherwork by others, making Tino's the one-stop leather shop. —*EL*

Trash & Vaudeville
4 St. Mark's Place between 2nd and 3rd Avenues
212-982-3590
M-Th: 12pm-8pm; F-Sa: 11:30am-8pm, Su: 1pm-7:30pm

TRASH & VAUDEVILLE IS SO PUNK IT HURTS. BUT who isn't on St. Marks? The store occupies a prime location that takes up two sprawling floors stocked with every kind of punk garb, from Old Skool to Ska to Goth, as well as some bondage treats like corsets and chain mail. Upstairs you'll find most of their menswear and streetwear for both sexes. Downstairs are the more upscale items, including men's suits and a decent selection of S/M attire, along with a shoe department bound to seduce even those who don't have a foot fetish.

While decidedly more Joey Ramone than Annie Sprinkle, Trash & Vaudeville is still good for a few turn-ons. Upstairs, their stunning array of schoolgirl minis ($50) in every tartan your heart and loins could desire is sure to stop you in your tracks. Another favorite is the Tripp studded halter in black pleather or red vinyl ($38) and hot pants to match ($32).

But for the real fun, you'll have to go down—downstairs, that is. Bypass the wall o'-T-shirts branded with every hardcore band imaginable and make your way to the racks of playwear. A couple of items to be found here are a rubber suit for him ($230 pants, $275 jacket) and an "open" dress with lace-up legs and bodice for her ($265), both by The Federation. You can also find some nice accessories of the whips' n' chains variety—collars, wristbands, belts—under the counters in the front.

Whatever you do, DO NOT skip the shoe section that occupies the back half of the lower level. This is by far Trash & Vaudeville's most solid offering. You'll find everything from flip-flops to fetish chaussures. Most of all, you'll find boots, boots, and more boots! Boots that buckle, slide, strap, or lace up as high as you fancy in every material imaginable: leather, pleather, rubber, glitter-sheathed, fur—the gang's all here. They'll take you higher with platforms, spikes, clodhoppers, cowboy and moon boots. Whether you're a cowpolk or a dom, coquette or space cadet, you'll find satisfaction. The truly fierce can pick up a set of heel covers with protruding spikes for extra edge (metal $100, rubber $50). And check out the bountiful (though jumbled) clearance area for a real steal, like a pair of platform, pony hair, calf boots for $170 (originally $279).

Since NYU is just around the corner Trash & Vaudeville caters as much to the after-school crowd as it does to the neighborhood lowlifes. This might account for their hardcore bag check and heavy staffing on the sales floor. There is little difference between the disaffected youth browsing and those minding the till. While prices are high at Trash & Vaudeville, quality is low (shoe department excepted), but the savvy shopper/sex kitten is sure to hone in on some good finds. —*SC*

Victoria's Secret

1981 Broadway at 67th Street
646-505-2280
M-Sa: 10am-9pm; Su: 11am-7pm
www.victoriasecret.com

THE REVOLVING DOOR HAD YET TO STOP SPINNING.
  "Can I help you?"
  "Can I help you?"
  "How can I help you?"
Such an overly aggressive sales force would have been

considered an annoyance in any other retail shop in the city, but not at Victoria's Secret on 67th Street and Broadway, where a selection of young saleswomen couldn't wait to service my girlfriend, Trixie, and me.

After we'd gawked at and groped (and sniffed, when Trix wasn't looking) nearly every article in stock, a tall, blonde saleswoman with Heidi-braids and a vaguely Scandinavian accent wafted over to mention that I could join her—Trixie that is—in the dressing room. Svetlana, for that was the blonde's name, was herself wearing a prominent lace number under a low-buttoned blouse.

We quickly gathered up the hottest underwear and nighties (red, black, see-through, lacey, and silky) from both floors. Svetlana insisted that we entertain some sexy (well, trashy) shoes to make Trixie even sexier/trashier.

The excitement builds. While I was sitting on a velvet settee, enjoying this private fashion show, Svetlana knocked on the door twice (we were in there for a while...you know...trying things out...I mean on), to ask if we needed help. Confession: What she asked was, "Can I do anything to help?" But what I heard was, "Can I do anything to help? Like adorn your girlfriend with a bra using only my teeth?" My fantasy response was "Yes, you can help. My girlfriend and I got a little carried away in here and now I can't seem to dislodge this underwire from my..."

After this experience, I know why Victoria's Secret keeps a first-class maintenance crew on permanent staff. Who knows what goes on behind closed doors?

The price: zippo. The fun: lots. The catch: none, except for one...and it's on the back of a brassiere. And best of all: Trixie thinks it was a hardship for me to join her on this pajama party because it was, after all, "shopping." I actually scored boyfriend points while defiling the couch in a Victoria's Secret fitting room. All around, it was an erotic and character-building experience.   —JT/MB

LEWD LITERATURE

THERE'S NOTHING QUITE LIKE CURLING UP WITH A good, juicy novel on a rainy day. The only thing better, of course, is curling up with a good, juicy, erotic novel—although in a pinch the *Kama Sutra* will do, as will vintage porn magazines. In fact, whatever turns your page will work just fine.

For all you fans of lewd and lascivious literature, take heart in knowing that New York boasts a number of specialty bookstores that cater to the connoisseur of erotica. Many of these shops carry top-shelf smut, not just the dime-store variety pulp romances that you can pick up at any newsstand. Whether you're looking for scorching novels, titillating comics, prurient poetry, vintage erotica, or the latest academic treatise on sadomasochism, the shops described below should be able to satisfy your desires.

So the next time you wake up on a Saturday morning to a symphony of raindrops kissing the pavement, don't fret that the sun is on hiatus. Just get your sorry ass out of bed, run to your nearest erotica bookstore, and pick up a book that tickles your fancy. Then haul your sorry ass back to bed where you can spend the rest of the day reading naughty words aloud to yourself or your lover. Who needs the sun anyway?

Bluestockings

172 Allen Street between Stanton and Rivington Streets
212-777-6028
Tu-Sa: noon-8pm; Su: 2pm-8pm ⚢

LOOKING FOR THE LATEST ISSUE OF *ON OUR Backs*? Missed an episode of Dyke TV? Then high-tail it to Blue Stockings, a small, women's bookstore and café that carries an inspired selection of female erotica—whether you take it lesbian, straight, or twisted. Named for the 18th-century women's literary society, Bluestockings opened in 1999 and is staffed almost entirely by volunteers. Most of the stock focuses on political and sexual issues, but there is also a collection of fiction, poetry, and non-fiction that you won't find anywhere else, such as *Faster Pussycats* by Trixi ($12.95), a chronicle of hot lesbian night life, *Gynomite: Fearless, Feminist Porn* edited by Liz Belile ($14.95), and *Femalia*, a collection of photography edited by Joani Blank that reveals the shocking truth that not all vaginas look alike.

Relax. The women running this bookstore are friendly and interesting and the atmosphere is comfortable, with flea-market couches and chairs for lounging and even line of stools at the counter. Get a cup of coffee ($1.25) and a Revolution Bar ($1.75), have a seat, and thumb through the latest issues of *Transgender Tapestry* or *Lesbian Connection*. You can also pick up some handy gift items, such as the Girls First Period Kit ($45) or a SuperDyke T-Shirt ($5).

Bluestockings sponsors a Lower East Side Women's Book Group as well as readings and lectures on a wide variety of topics. This is the only bookstore in New York City that caters exclusively to women, and being a few short blocks from Meow Mix and Toys in Babeland doesn't hurt. Here you can prop *The Whole Lesbian Sex Book* by Felice Newman ($21.95) on your lap without feeling an ounce of embarrassment—try that in Barnes & Noble—and if you're lucky, you just might pick up a nice Jewish girl to bring home to mother. —*HT*

Creative Visions

548 Hudson Street between Charles and Perry Streets
212-645-7573
Su-Th: noon-10pm; F-Sa: noon-11pm
www.creativevisionsbooks.com

LOCATED IN THE WEST VILLAGE, THIS IS A LIFE-style bookshop designed for gay and lesbian tastes. It's bright, breezy, and broad in range with an emphasis on general literature and non-fiction. But there's a large selection of fiction, too, including everything from the classics (James Baldwin) to contemporary reads (try

EROTIC

Maupin's *The Night Listener*), and anything not on the shelves can be ordered. Lots of mouth-watering visuals take your attention from the books, however. Recent coffee-table glossies are featured everywhere (e.g., *Dream Boys II*) along with the usual fleshy calendars and PC's of studs and chicks with the right things in the right places. There's a large mystery/crime section for those who just want to curl up with a swarthy detective, and there's a load of material on spiritu-

Hot Off the Press

IT SHOULD COME AS NO SURPRISE THAT NEW YORK, the mainstream media capital of the world, is also the erotic media capital of the world. The city boasts a wide array of raunchy TV shows, websites, and print publications that cater to every whim and fetish of Gotham's denizens. Even venerable WBAI, best known for its political programming, recently launched a sex-themed radio show called *Erotoradio*, which airs on Mondays at midnight.

While Silicon Alley flounders, the New York-based online sex and dating industry continues to boom. A web search on "sex" and "New York" spews forth a multitude of tantalizing digital treats including www.tantranewyork.com, where you can be coached in the ancient art of Tantric sex, and www.ny-exotics.com, a virtual red light district for wannabe johns, where you can look at scores of photos of potential companions before plunking down the big bucks for the big night.

For singles (and the not so single) on the prowl who prefer online titillation and email foreplay to a conventional lunch date, there are numerous sites—including MatchDoctor.com, FriendFinder.com, lavalife.com, Match.com, and nerve.com—that are literally loaded with members from New York City. The best local dating site, hands down, is nerve.com, where the sexually irreverent mix with witty perverts and digital exhibitionists. Although all the sites let you sign up for free, expect to pay a premium for "extra" services, which could be as basic as replying to another member's ad. The pluses of online dating include stalker-free (well, nearly) interaction, the ability to search for those features that you most covet (such as, say, extremely long nostril

ality and gay relationships. There are also plenty of erotic comics (crammed with obscenely-built torsos) and even a cookbook or two (think *The Naked Chef*).

Want something for tonight that's a little bit more rousing? Choose from the bounty of boy videos lavishly spread on the far wall, and a whisper of girl vids (many with a socio/politico/documentary leaning), located with the lesbian-related stuff. Videos are $4.

hair), and private chat rooms for one-on-one anonymous action.

nerve.com is also the local nexus for erotic literature and culture. With a combination of well written, titillating articles, softcore photo essays, and sexy member surveys, you can have your mind and your libido equally inspired. Salon.com, which resembles nerve in the quality and style of writing, requires members to pay a fee to access the truly juicy articles.

For you TV addicts, Channel 35 on the Time Warner cable system is legendary for its late night lineup of tacky, spicy commercials (nothing more than erotic loops featuring strippers and snippets of porn) and locally oriented sex talk shows. Robin Byrd, an ex-porn star and host of the long running *Robin Byrd Show*, features male and female, veteran and up-and-coming strippers (many of whom also appear in porn films). The show airs on Tuesdays at 10pm, Thursdays at 11pm, and Saturdays at 10:30pm and 1am, and is repeated endlessly in the wee hours of the morning. Other not-to-be-missed Emmy-worthy shows include *Men for Men*, *Temptations*, *Spicy Stuff*, and the grand daddy of them all, Al Goldstein's *Midnight Blue*.

For those of you who actually still read, the standard hetero sex rag is *Screw Magazine* which is published weekly and provides a wealth of information on the New York sex scene as well as reviews of porn films and a host of trashy articles. Most of the other local sexzines are merely fronts for advertising escort services, strip clubs, and the like. *The New York Press*, *Time Out New York*, and the *Village Voice* all have weekly sex columnists who provide some useful advice as well as a great deal of comic relief. For a glimpse of what's going on in the gay sex world, pick up a copy of *H/X* magazine. It's free and can be found in numerous gay-friendly boutiques. —MU

Having a same-sex matrimonial moment? Thoughtfully available are groom-with-groom and bride-with-bride wedding-cake figures, along with the usual novelty knick-knacks and point-of-sale items for quick "darling, how cute!" gifts—though the place doesn't extend to your leather hoods, fancy dildos, or dental dams. Remember, it's a serious bookstore.

A big bonus for the boys who are into vintage titillation: boxes stacked with retro photographs of burly men from the '50s through the early '80s—there are men wrestling, men bodybuilding, men comfortably fisting in good ol' fashioned slings. Best finds are the original snaps of sweet amateur models, eager to make an impression on some future porn producer. Photos: small $5, large $10. Also available are vintage magazines such as Playgirl and Stroke, and a collection of CD's. —*TM*

Midtown Comics
200 West 40th Street between 7th and 8th Avenues
212-302-8192
M-Sa: 11am-9pm; Su: 12pm-7pm
www.midtowncomics.com

I DON'T CARE HOW MANY CULTURAL STUDIES Ph.D. candidates carry on about the artistic merit and contemporary themes contained within a comic book—I mean graphic novel—they are still not that sexy. And neither, generally, are the people who read them. I challenge anyone to walk into a comic shop and be overcome with desire to make mad, passionate love with the type of clientele that salivates over the latest installment of *X-Men*. I'm guessing that the plastic slipcover on said comics is the closest thing most of these fan boys and girls are going to get to a bit of prophylactic action. But perhaps that's just me since judging by the numbers of people poring over the illustrated fantasy magazines and hard-core Japanese adult *manga*, not everyone shares my views.

Midtown Comics carries a reasonable collection of both illustrated and photographic porn with a small erotic art section. There is also a range of fetish publications available, as well as some trusty back issues of *Playboy*. Buying your porn from Midtown Comics has the added advantage of avoiding those unsightly retailer's names on your credit card statement, although personally, I'd feel less embarrassed if people knew I shopped regularly at Harry's House of Hard Core, or Barry's Boutique of Butt. But again, that's just me. —SS

New York Body Archive

9 9h Avenue, 2nd Floor (near 13th Street)
212-807-6441 (for information)
718-338-9546 (to make an appointment)
By appointment only (There is a sliding scale for research beginning at $25/hour with a two-hour minimum per visit.)
body ny@aol.com

SNAKING YOUR WAY UP THE DIMLY LIT, RECTUM-like stairwell of the New York Body Archive, you might be tempted to turn back, what with ominous candles and warning signs lining the way. But don't, because this establishment offers ties that bind—and gag—and much, much more.

The New York Body Archive, founded by renowned body modifier Matty Jankowski is a combined research center, library, gift shop, and spectacle. A book-burning fanatic would have a field day here. The Archive offers books and magazines about (deep breath) tattooing, piercing, body modification, branding, scarification, blood play, fetish, S/M and B&D, mehandi/henna and body painting. Also for sale are custom and ethnic body jewelry, clothing, hard-core dishware, tickle videos, records, whips—you name it! If it's about sex, it's here at the Body Archive.

The Archive sponsors lectures, stages live performances

(join the free email list to receive invitations to special events and performances), and offers consulting services. It's a great place to browse, ogle, and go home with something to hang over a mantelpiece, like an 18th- century body harness.

The Archive is for everyone, including: closet deviants hoping to uncover some new ways to please—or tease—their partner (or themselves); cultural anthropologists researching the history of body modification; human sexuality educators needing to brush up on the latest sex practices and trends; and dominatrixes needing advice on preparing a master-slave contract.

When I asked Matty to show me something really shocking, he reached for a book on the history of enemas. (Wait a minute…that goes where? And does what?)

Yup, there's plenty to see in this small, stimulating space, so swing by the Body Archive to learn something new. —*JT*

Personal Pleasures

WHATEVER YOUR PLEASURE, SPANKING OR wanking, New York's print and electronic media can match you up with a willing mate. *The New York Press* and *The Village Voice* are free tabloids that can be found on countless street corners—stacked neatly inside colorful plastic boxes. In both papers, the personals are located toward the back, appropriately near the seemingly infinite ads for escort services.

The New York Press' "Variations" section (free to place 30-word ad in paper and website (www.nypress.com); $2.19 per minute to respond with voicemail message) suits those with liberated libidos. Beginners might refer to the helpful abbreviation key: TV=transvestite, OTK=over the knee, and UTB=up the butt. Here's a sampling: "Attractive male with 25 years experience in administering erotic spankings, has psychology background." With no shortage of man-on-man talent, one poetical ad asked, "Nuts about Nuts. Do you have a pair that loves to be licked, sucked and stroked?" Under the Whatever's Clever category "Hot guy 4 strap-on" precedes "Seeking a sincere Bi married guy who will share wife's worn and dirty panties."

Roger's Time Machine

207 West 14th Street between 7th and 8th Avenues
212-691-0380

M, Tu, Th: 12pm-7pm; W, F, Sa: 11am-7.30pm; Su: 1pm-6pm

VINTAGE EROTICA COMPRISES ONLY A SMALL PART of the stock at Roger's Time Machine; the rest of the collection consists largely of back-issue comic books. However, sex sells, and the shop brings in a tidy sum trafficking faded *Playboy* and *Penthouse* magazines.

An entertaining time can be had poring over the coy, illustrated covers of the '50s, the sultry, modish cover girls of the '60s and the buxom, seductively smiling '70s nymphets. But far greater entertainment is to be derived from the more obscure publications on offer—mags such

The Village Voice (free to place a 6-line personal ad in paper and on website (www.villagevoice.com/personal); $1.95 per minute to respond with voicemail message) attracts an equally fetishistic following. Categories include: "Multiples," which attracts listings like "A1 Hot Couple, Stacked Asian and Well Endowed Black Male"; "Transgender," ("She-male wanted"); and the catchall "Anything Goes" with heady headers like "More Please! Ouch! It hurts! More Please!"

If your taste runs more missionary than masochistic, consider www.nerve.com (free to browse and post an ad; 30 minutes of instant messaging costs two credits; credits sold in packages: 25 for $19.95, 60 for $34.95, 120 for $49.95) where thousands of young singles post personals—many with pictures. Attracting an educated crowd of writers, musicians, lawyers, and Internet execs—many of them local—nerve.com makes it easy (and addictive) to click through the masses. Not all ads are tempting. Stunningly sophomoric postings include, "Most of all, I want someone who is cool to hang with!!! If your [sic] uptight and a total bitch I don't want to know you," and "If you are horny enough or cool enough to jump on me the minute we meet—that works for me too." Don't miss the boards with heated banter on pubic hair, masturbation, and sex toys. —*LDP*

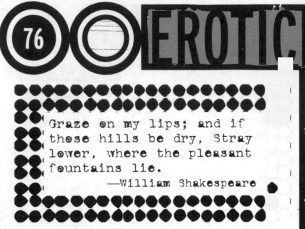

> Graze on my lips; and if
> those hills be dry, Stray
> lower, where the pleasant
> fountains lie.
> —William Shakespeare

as *Gent* ("Home of the D Cup" where "Life begins at 40 (inches)") or *Daring* (which proclaims "Women love a man with bed power") are well worth checking out.

For those with nothing to fear, but gear itself, there are the magazines for the nudists among us. But Roger's collection is not just about titillation. There are many items that lean toward the instructional. The March '75 issue of *All Man* puts KY into DIY with advice on how to build an orgy room. *Daring* also endeavors to educate. In one issue, bed power meets girl power in a feature that questions whether marijuana use leads to the growth of male bosoms. For those who prefer to give rather than receive, Roger is always on the lookout for early gay porn, those thinly disguised muscle magazines from the '50s and '60s. So, if you wish to further investigate the bed power movement, and if you like your porn a little tongue in cheek, take a trip in Roger's Time Machine.   —*SS*

Village Comics

214 Sullivan St. between Bleecker and W. 3rd Streets
212-777-2770

M-Tu: 10:30am-7:30pm; W-Sa: 10:30am-8:30pm; Su: 11am-7pm
www.villagecomics.com
www.villageerotica.com (adults only)

WHY ON EARTH WOULD WE LIST A COMIC SHOP IN an erotic guide? Are we perverse or what? Well, the fact is that we were innocently walking down 6th Avenue when a young woman handed us a neon orange flyer. We assumed it was an announcement for a clothing sale or some other innocuous event, but upon closer inspection it turned out to be a hot photo of porn star Jasmine St. Claire, who was scheduled to appear at, of all places, Village Comics. Our curiosity sufficiently aroused, we immediately strolled over to Sullivan Street.

Village Comics, in business for over 18 years, has perhaps the most comprehensive and unusual inventory we've ever seen. Their aim is to provide a true fantasy world for every age, and based on our visit, we'd have to call their efforts an unqualified success. They have, of course, plenty of classic and contemporary comics and trading cards geared towards kids as well as a vast array of sci-fi, horror, and fantasy art books. But Village Comics also stocks an enormous collection of current and vintage adult magazines, comics, art books, and lithographs, as well as sexy and realistic model kits and statues such as the pre-painted porcelain Pleasure Seeker in bondage gear for $89.95.

In the book section, Swimsuit Sweeties cuddles up next to Tolkien and in the build-it-yourself model section, Star Wars characters peep across the aisle at Japanese nymphettes. In the "adults-only" section, the hottest items are the new ICONS series by Taschen, at $10 apiece. Where does one begin with the comics? There are Eurotica and Amerotica titles, anime, Spanish imports Kiss Comix and Wet Comix, Eros Comix, and Japanese manga erotica, ranging in price from $1.95 to $45 and up. Comic book artists such as Kevin Taylor, Barry Blair, Colin Chan, Roberto Baldazzini, Jack Munroe, and Milo Manara fill the burgeoning shelves. But don't stop there. There are also current and back issues of *Playboy, Hustler, Busty,* and *Gent,* as well as Priaprism Press graphic novels and the fetish photography of Eric Kroll. Village Comics also carries adult videos, from adult anime to fetish videos guaranteed to scratch every itch.

While it's definitely straight-guy oriented, there was at least one woman browsing the shelves while we were there, perhaps shopping for a gift for a male friend. Sounds like the perfect stocking-stuffer to us! —*SS*

Virgin Megastore

52 East 14th Street at Broadway
212-598-4666
M-Sa: 9am-1am; Su: 10am-midnight

1540 Broadway between 45th and 46th Streets
212-921-1020
Su-Th: 9am-1am; F-Sa: 9am-2am
www.virginmega.com

VIRGIN MEGASTORE HAS BECOME SUCH A HOUSE-
hold name that it seems no puerile joy can any longer be
derived from its utterance. What a shame. But if making
your first foray into erotic multimedia, Virgin is a reasonable place to start. While it may be best known for its large
collection of musical CDs and the hours of free fun to be
had at the countless listening stations scattered throughout the store, also on offer is a goodly range of erotic
books, DVDs, and videos.

For those who desire the stimulation of the printed
word, the well-stocked erotica and sexuality bookcases
provide anthologies of heterosexual, bisexual, and gay
tales; a wide range of how-to guides; and a few respectable
coffee table works of fetish photography. The aisles are
spacious and the crowds tend to be thin, so you can actually browse at your leisure without some pervert peering
over your shoulder.

If you're accustomed to watching porn flicks on your
trusty VCR, you'll want to run out and buy a DVD player
right away. With DVD technology, you pick the camera
angle, location, and position. Heck, you can even pick the
orifice. At Virgin, you'll find fine classics such as
Interactive Sex Party. The simulated sex on a DVD is so
good that you might even retire your blow-up dolly.

The video collection here is small, and like the DVDs,
is largely pitched to a male, heterosexual audience. There
is, however, a very small gay and lesbian collection, ranging from art-house trusties such as *My Own Private Idaho*
to steam-house trusties, like *Boy Babe Frenzy*. —SS

EROTIC ART & ARTISTS

JUST WHAT IS EROTIC ART? AND HOW, IF AT ALL, DOES it differ from pornography? We can't give you a pat answer to those questions and we're certainly not interested in launching into a long-winded academic discussion on the subject, but what we can say is that we think we know the real thing when we see it. The talented New York visual artists listed below—along with a rather unique gallery—are definitely offering the real thing—the kind of art that's unfortunately often kept under wraps.

The work we reviewed—which includes sculpture, jewelry, prints, photographs, and video—can be characterized as stylish, intelligent, innovative, funky, fun, and titillating—and sometimes as all of the above. Here you'll find Eros in photographic portraits of the woman next door; in Mother Earth's natural forms; and in videotapes of couples at play. But don't accept our word for it. Take a close look for yourself, check out the artist's websites, and if you like what you see, consider making an appointment to view the work up close and in person. Just think how cool it would be to own a piece of bona fide erotic art. But don't forget to hide it when your folks come to visit. —*TH*

EROTIC

Barbara Nitke

www.barbaranitke.com

BEFORE YOU ENTER BARBARA NITKE'S ONLINE gallery, you must agree to a statement that you "are not offended by photographic depictions of the nude human form or of human sexuality." That's because Ms. Nitke, a respected photographer with a large following and twenty years of experience, pulls no punches with her work. Whether in stark black-and-white or absorbing color, each of her shots goes into explicit detail: Everything from the suggestion of a kiss to the aftermath of the sexual act—not to mention all the stuff in between—is represented. (There's a substantial section devoted to bondage in its various forms.)

The artist got her first exposure to sexual images through her ex-husband who was a producer of porn films. So when Ms. Nitke took up photography, the subject matter seemed a natural fit. Indeed, some of her "American Ecstasy" series uses the adult film industry as its setting and inspiration: "Supergirls Do General Hospital, I" finds a half-clothed woman on a gurney (no doubt she'll soon be playing doctor); "Nina, Damian and Henri" shows one actress getting ready for her close-up; another one gets a mouthful in "Blair Castle in Piggies." The gamut of human emotions, says Ms. Nitke, is what she's trying to capture. Sex, she explains, is that window into a person's soul.

Print prices range from $750 to $2,000. They can be purchased either by contacting the artist at barbara@barbaranitke.com or via her local gallery, Clampart (250 West 27th Street, New York, NY 10001; 646-230-0020, www.clampart.com). For commissioned works, contact Ms. Nitke via email. Prices start at $2,500.   —MRB

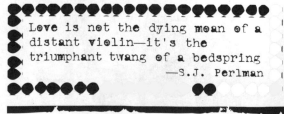

Love is not the dying moan of a distant violin—it's the triumphant twang of a bedspring
—S.J. Perlman

Erotics Gallery

41 Union Square West, Suite 1011 at 17th Street
212-633-2241
M-F: noon-5pm, by appointment only
www.eroticrarities.com
eroticrarities@att.net

"CAKES!" GROANS EDIE SOLOW, INTO THE PHONE. "People ask the operator where they can find erotic cakes, and they always get referred to me." No, you won't find "hot" baked goods at Erotics Gallery, but other sweet spots are assured satisfaction at the city's premier dealer in adult artifacts. Erotics Gallery hit the web a few years ago, but a trek to its Union Square digs may still be in order.

Solow, a transplanted Oklahoman with plainspoken charm, gives good chat (particularly if you're punctual in keeping your appointment). Samples from her international collection, which she started amassing with her former husband in the mid-'70s, are there for the viewing. The fornicating frogs always get a reaction from first-time guests to her gallery-cum-office, a pleasant, unpretentious space for connoisseurs of the carnal.

Suggestively shaped jewelry ("fun, not functional") is her latest passion. Flipping through her catalogs, you find an array of articles, from erotically carved meerschaum pipes and walking sticks to porn posters and beautifully stylized prints depicting all varieties of passion. Prices range from $20 to what Solow calls "unmentionable." Credit card purchases may be made through the website, which features a "cybercatalog" spanning three centuries of adults-only art.

Perched above Union Square, Erotics Gallery began as a shop on Christopher Street in 1975. Customer interest energized its development, says Solow, noting "It's a constant work in progress. The concept was so new back then that no one knew what to make of it, not even myself, but now the sale of erotic art…is normal to me. It's all about play and fantasy, and the gallery does respond to what customers want." So there are no cakes here (and no photography, either; "that's a whole other realm" says Edie), but there are plenty of other goodies to sink your teeth into. —RC

Heather Firth Fine Art Photography

www.heatherfirth.com

THINK OF HEATHER FIRTH AS A TOPOGRAPHIC-ally-minded Georgia O'Keefe—with a really good pair of hiking boots. Ms. Firth is the woman behind "Earth Erotica," a stunning series of color photographs that illustrate found sexual imagery in nature: the curves of rocks, the suggestive slopes of stones, and the primal peaks and valleys of mountains and deserts. To discover these provocative images, she trots the globe—from New York to California and from Italy to Jordan—allowing neither rain nor sleet nor snow to interfere with her quest.

Ms. Firth's background as a sex educator has no doubt played some role in inspiring her pursuit of Eros in nature. Her imagery remains subtly ambiguous so that the viewer

The Mother of All

IT WAS 1968 IN NEW YORK CITY WHEN BETTY DODSON first went public with her love of sex with a one-woman exhibition of her erotic drawings. She was both the artist and the model. Her classical nudes were rendered so exquisitely that the exhibition sold out. It was at this time that Dodson earned the reputation of hosting the best sex parties in town. She was troubled, however, by the fact that far too many women were faking orgasm to please men. Her group sex experiences convinced her that the repression and guilt surrounding masturbation was at the heart of sexual repression. For her next exhibition, Dodson showed two larger than life nudes happily masturbating to orgasm. Although there was a media blackout of the show and nothing sold, Dodson came to the conclusion that teaching

is afforded an equal thrill of discovery: In any given landscape, you might perceive the curve of a buttock, the crevice between two thighs, a phallic sculpture…or, you might just find a stunning formation of stone. As one observer quipped, "These photos rock!" Whatever your interpretation, Ms. Firth manages to stimulate the mind—and perhaps a few other parts of the anatomy as well.

Unframed color prints range in size from 8-by-10 to 20-by-30 inches, and start at $195. For inquiries, visit www.heatherfirth.com. —*MRB*

Melissa Ulto

www.thecataract.com
multo@multo.com
917-549-7006

IF YOUR IDEA OF EROTICA IS A BONY BARELY-LEGAL lass, Ms. Ulto's work may not resonate with you. But if you delight in seeing a female in full—striking, beautiful women with fire in their hearts, curiousity in their eyes, and curves in their bodies—then unMade Movie is a must-see.

women how to have orgasms would be her feminist commitment.

In 1973, Dodson left the art world to facilitate sexuality workshops and became the first public spokesperson for the joys and benefits of guilt-free masturbation, which she espoused in an article in *Ms. Magazine*. Her groundbreaking book, *Liberating Masturbation*, was self-published in 1974 and soon became an underground classic. Dodson traveled across the country lecturing and running workshops, during which she would teach women to become orgasmic through masturbation.

Sex for One: The Joy of Selfloving, was published in 1987, revised in 1996, and has helped bring Dodson's work to a much wider audience. *Orgasms for Two* will be available in the fall of 2002. *Dodson holds a Ph.D.* in sexology and maintains a private practice in New York City. Visit her website at www.bettydodson.com. —*MC*

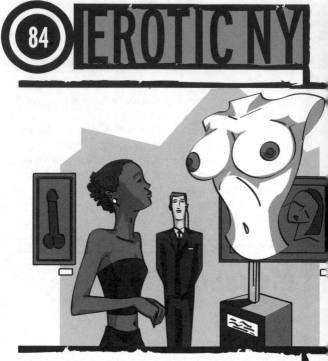

New York-based Melissa Ulto is a self-described inter-disciplinary artist—poet, videographer, photographer, painter, and writer—responsible for this online exhibit of sexually charged digital images. More suggestive than explicit, more R-rated than NC-17, Ms. Ulto's photos draw on B-movies and pulp fiction filtered through the lens of cyber culture (it's a collection, clearly, that benefits from the immediacy and changeability of its internet environment). With subtitles like "the dreaded red head," "pink aphrodite," "girlfriends," "sugar," "fair addiction" (in which both Marilyn Monroe and Tippi Hedren are evoked), and "platinum," Ms. Ulto's work portrays women (and a few men) in a variety of states of dress and emo-tion: lounging in lingerie, stretched catlike on a pile of unmade linens, eyes rimmed with kohl and lips luscious-ly stained. Interestingly, all of her subjects seem aware they're being watched—many of them address the camera directly—which affords the viewer something of a per-sonal connection with each image. Ms. Ulto's brief, verse captions serve as dialogue for unMade Movie, and thank-

The Museum of Sex

THE MUSEUM OF SEX IS DEVOTED TO ALL ASPECTS of human sexuality, and its inaugural exhibit, "NYC Sex: How New York City Transformed Sex in America," is a prime example of the breadth and depth to which this newly opened institution aspires. The exhibit covers such varied topics as the city's market in illegal abortions and black market condoms, the city's first sex scandal, the emergence of a gay subculture at the turn of the century, the beginnings of S/M culture in the '30s, Stonewall, AIDS, AIDS activism and— phew— that's not all. Art, historic ephemera, documentary photographs (including work by Annie Sprinkle and Harvey Wang), historic birth control devices, fetish garments, vintage stag films, and choice items from the Kinsey Institute will all be part of the exhibit. The Museum, in fact, has been granted unlimited access to the Institute's archives — so patrons can expect to see a lot of fascinating Kinsey items housed in future exhibits as well.

Founded by Dan Gluck, a young software entrepreneur, the idea for such a museum was conceived when a friend suggested the idea over cocktails. Gluck spent the next four years fundraising, assembling a curatorial, archival, and business staff, and amassing an impressive list of museum advisors, including June Reinisch, the Director Emeritus of the Kinsey Institute, and Jan Seidler Ramirez, the Museum Director of the New York Historical Society.

The Museum plans on publishing a companion volume to its "NYC Sex" exhibition. It will feature sexy conversations (or rather, conversation about sex) between prominent New Yorkers, including the Pulitzer Prize-winning author/artist Art Spiegelman, performance artist Karen Finley, porn star Vanessa Del Rio, happy hooker Xavier Hollander, and Gene Simmons from Kiss.

So just imagine: New York City's very own cultural institution dedicated to the history and continuing evolution of human sexuality. How great is that? Who wouldn't want to spend a long Saturday being intellectually, culturally, and—just maybe—sexually stimulated? And if that weren't enough, partial proceeds from the Museum will go to benefit the AIDS Community Research Initiative of America. It all kinda makes a person proud to call New York City home. —SL

233 5th Avenue at 27th Street
www.museumofsex.com

fully, the "film" suggests it's far from finished. We eagerly await the next installment.

Unframed prints are $150 (8" x 11") and $250 (13" x 19"); framed pricing available upon request. The artist can be commissioned for portraits. Contact her at the email address or phone number listed above. —*MRB*

Michael Berkowitz Photography

212-868-3661
Call for an appointment
www.michaelberkowitz.com
michaeljayberkowitz@yahoo.com

A PROFESSIONAL PAINTER AND SCULPTOR FOR OVER 25 years, Berkowitz's work has been exhibited in many museums and private galleries throughout the country. But this artist has also been taking photographs for over 30 years, work that he has not exhibited until now.

Winner of the 2001 New York Camera Club Award, Berkowitz now devotes most of his creative energy to photographing the nude female form. He draws much of his inspiration from French erotic photography, as well as E. J. Bellocq's portraits of prostitutes in early 20th century New Orleans—later known as the Storyville portraits.

He aims to capture the sensual female form of the "real" women that surround us—silicon breasts and model-slim bodies don't especially interest him. On the other hand, breasts that are too small or a butt that is too large by society's standards are the imperfections that Berkowitz believes creates the beauty of a woman. He finds his own personal idea of beauty within each model and then attempts to capture that beauty on film.

Berkowitz's photos are as much about portraiture and each model's particularity as they are about the nude human figure. Although the photos might be considered erotic by some, ultimately the images are simply about form

and beauty. Each photograph presents a heightened, almost surreal level of detail and texture. The model is typically shot in a stylized, fantasy bedroom evocative of the 1920s.

If you're interested in being photographed, call him directly to discuss the possibilities. Often, he is willing to barter with models—for example, exchanging permission to exhibit and sell his work for a set of proofs (which of course can be enlarged).

You can view some of Michael's work at www.michaelberkowitz.com. —*KM*

Ordinary Films
212-956-3226
www.ordinary-films.com
info@ordinary-films.com

MARIE AND JACK ARE MARRIED AND VERY MUCH IN love. And despite the vicious rumor that marriage dulls the sexual appetite, Marie and Jack are extremely attracted to each other, and they really want to show it—on tape. They are the subjects of *Marie and Jack: A Love Story*, the tamely named XXX video that is the brainchild of Ordinary Films, a New York City-based outfit taking a new approach to video porn.

If you're tired of the usual porn with its trite and tired plots (knock, knock—the well-hung delivery boy is at the door delivering his load of groceries to the sexually frustrated housewife) then Marie and Jack, the first in Ordinary Films' line of real people/real sex videos, is the answer to your lustful prayers. Instead of porn starlets with boob jobs and cheesy production values, Ordinary Films' oeuvre features actual married couples shot documentary style, both talking about what arouses them and then demonstrating their coital activities for the cameras with no holds barred. You can expect to see the prerequisite amount of genuflecting before genitalia, but there is both great attention to production values and development of narrative. Surprisingly, the presence of narrative doesn't sabotage the sex, rather, it makes what you see on screen more watchable and highly appropriate for the sort of couple's viewing that won't insult the intelligence.

You can sample some clips of Marie and Jack from Ordinary Films' website, and you can also order the 30-minute video there for $19.95. Check their website for information on upcoming titles, or if you're really feeling spirited, to find out how to become the subject of an Ordinary Film. 15 minutes of fame, here you come... —*AT*

Rene Iatba Akau
130 Dupont Street between Manhattan Avenue and McGuiness Boulevard
Brooklyn
718-389-5631
vze3bmwr@verizon.net

RENE HAS BEEN A FIXTURE OF THE NEW YORK ART scene for decades, known for his Muhammed Ali-esque tagline, "I Am the Best Artist," and for site-specific "events" at the Museum of Modern Art, which take aim at what he perceives to be the hypocrisy and commercial nature of the art establishment.

The focus of his work is primarily the vulva, which he carves in wood, paints in oils and acrylics, sculpts in clay, and draws using various media. Rene believes the image of the vulva is sacred, and frequently renders it at the center of the cross and on mythical landscapes. He celebrates a part of the human anatomy that has been vilified for centuries, and yet is what he considers to be "the seat of all human creativity." And after listening to Rene expound his philosophy of art and sexuality, the depth of meaning in his work—which projects a unique transcendent beauty—becomes even more apparent than at first glance.

A profound social critic, feminist, and artistic pioneer. Rene prefers to sell his work to individuals who understand the philosophy behind it and who are interested in commissioning pieces. If you fit the bill, a visit to Rene's studio and private gallery space in Brooklyn is in order. —*MU*

ADULT TOY STORES

REMEMBER WHEN YOU WERE A LITTLE KID AND A TRIP to the toy store seemed just like heaven on earth? Remember how you'd run through the aisles with your chums, checking out all the latest gizmos, gadgets, games, and dolls—wishing with all your might that you had enough spare change to buy everything in the store? And remember how after a successful shopping expedition you couldn't wait to get home to unwrap your bundles and play with the newest additions to your toy collection? Well now that you're older (you best be over 18 if you're reading this), you may find that a visit to an adult toy store will bring back those same happy childhood memories. And if it does, we suggest you immediately stop what you're doing and find a good shrink because let's face it, Parcheesi and butt plugs have absolutely nothing in common and you're going to need some serious help. Psychology aside, adult toy stores are a joy to visit, especially with a partner. Even if you don't buy anything, the sheer entertainment value of contemplating the varied uses of a blow-up doll or a love swing, makes the trip well worth it. Heck, this one little trip might even save your relationship.

The shops listed below are essentially erotic department stores since they stock everything you might possibly need for a spicy evening out on the town, or a sizzling night at home. You'll find videos, lotions, lingerie, fetishwear, vibrators, novelties, books, condoms, and much more, but expect the selection—with the exception of toys such as vibrators and dildos—to be inferior to that of a specialty store that focuses on one area of the erotic repertoire. This is one-stop shopping in the true American tradition, which is not only great in terms of convenience, but is also a godsend for folks who turn red when renting a porno at their local video store or get embarrassed when buying condoms. At the shops below, you can rest assured that everybody is looking for a little nookie-enhancement, so there's no need to be self-conscious. Prices tend to vary widely so it is best to comparison shop before purchasing. Also some of the stores sell via mail order so you don't have to worry about coming back to the office after lunch hiding an 18-inch-double dildo. —*TH*

EROTIC

A & J Lingerie (NDC)

41 West 28th Street between Broadway & 6th Avenue
212-689-2415
M-F: 9am-7pm; Sa: 9am-5pm
lingerienyc@aol.com

TUCKED AWAY ON THE SECOND FLOOR OF A NONDESCRIPT building in the garment district are probably the greatest bargains you'll find in erotic merchandise. Run by a charming mother and son team, and operating on the principle of volume sales, A & J sells both wholesale and retail, and stocks a full line of body stockings, baby dolls, bras, panties, and some regular junior clothing. In the back room, of course, you'll find the real goods: vibrators, dolls, novelties (ever sip from a penis straw?), games, handcuffs—plus some kick-ass shoes. (In the case of the thigh-high, spiked-heel vinyl boots, you can take that literally.)

The prices alone are orgasmic. Stockings and thigh-highs range from $2-$7; body stockings from $4.75-$16; and matching bra & panty sets from $8 (including some hot black vinyl numbers which would go nicely with the boots). The top seller in the lingerie department is a thong with feather-puffs on the sides (they also feature an "emergency" unhook closure), a steal at $2.50. Edible undies and candy condoms start at $3. Another steady seller are his and hers underwear sets, from $14-$21. You'll also find 3-piece sets (bra, thong, and regular panties) as low as $28, selling elsewhere for $70. A&J has lots of baby-doll sets, in all styles and colors, ranging from $17. Long sheer gown & panty sets go for $26-$38. Don't overlook the garters for (yes, this is a direct quote) "little mamas" ($6.75) and ibig mamasî ($8.40).

In the back room (where the proprietor assured me they don't allow children), you can find super-high, open-toe NYLA shoes starting at $20. The above-mentioned thigh-high vinyl boots start at around $60. Back here is also where you'll find penis straws ($5 per dozen), testicle-shaped ice-cube trays ($2.25), furry handcuffs ($11), regular handcuffs ($4.75), genital and nipple jewelry ($7-$11), plus a host of games, creams, and other novelties. The best deal to be had, though, are the vibrators at a

ridiculous $7-$14. The same models (such as the Rabbit, made famous by *Sex and the City*), sell at other shops for quadruple the price.

For fabulous bargains (sold by really nice, decent people), you can't do better than   —*A&J*

Come Again
353 East 53rd Street between 1st and 2nd Avenues
212-308-9394
M-F: 11am-7pm; Sa: 11am-6pm
www.comeagainnyc.com

COME AGAIN IS THE TYPE OF PLACE WHERE FRAT boys buy crotchless panties for their girlfriends and women go to pick up gag gifts for their best friend's bachelorette party. Novelty items dominate the cramped L-shaped store which is home to all things penis-shaped: penis lollipops ($1 each), gummies ($5.95 per bag), water guns (mini-peepee for $3.95, $8.95 for a full schlong),

pecker earrings that glow in the dark ($3.95 pair), and assorted corsages featuring, you guessed it, penises ($14.95 each). Water bottles, whistles, cake pans, ice cube trays…the list goes on. There's even a penile take on the arrow-through-the-head gag and a Groucho Marx mask with a priapic nose.

One retreat from this throng of dongs is the lingerie section, just off to the left as you enter the store. Two racks in the center of the room are jammed with a surfeit of overpriced and poorly made clothing (mostly nylon and polyester), including teddies and uniforms (mostly schoolgirl). All items are wrapped in protective plastic, like your grandmother's couch. Some racier vinyl items— bodices, skirts, hot pants—line the outer walls. (I was after a red PVC bra but couldn't find anything larger than a C cup.) For men, you'll find G-strings featuring animal faces with elongated noses ($14.95 each).

At the back of the store there's a moderate selection of vibrators and dildos boxed and crammed into floor-to-ceiling shelves alongside blow-up dolls, model vaginas and anuses, penis pumps, plus cock rings, condoms, and lube. There are more vibrators behind the counter that can be tested out, but I didn't feel comfortable asking, having been followed around the store by a salesperson who kept repeating "May I help you?" in a suspicious tone as if I were a mall rat on a shoplifting mission. Meanwhile, another clerk chided a customer for flipping through the books, suggesting he make do with the descriptions on the back covers rather than crack the spines. That's too bad since the store's saving grace is its strong book selection. Come Again carries more than just pulp and porn for the boudoir biblio-phile. I would dare to call it a miniature Strand, offering adult comic books, imported magazines, how-to guides, S&M and fetish titles, and erotica of many sub-genres (women's, gay, lesbian, bisexual—even Victorian). Best buys are in the used bin, from which you can pick up retro pulp like Nora's Liquid Lips at $3 a pop or 4 books for $10. Videos can also be found in this area, though most are packed so tightly into bins it's difficult to browse.

For a sex shop, Come Again doesn't do much to pro-mote an erotic ambiance. Between the suspicious staff and poorly displayed merchandise I found it difficult to get in the mood. The autographed glossies of female porn stars on the wall behind the counter reinforce the store's male slant and the S&M harnesses hanging alongside them appear to be more for show than for play. But give the store credit, it's been in business for 19 years and in this city, that's no easy feat. —*SC*

Eve's Garden

119 West 57th Street (Suite 1201) between 6th and 7th Avenues
M-Sa: 11 am-7pm
212-757-8651
www.evesgarden.com

INCONGRUOUSLY, THIS SEX TOY STORE IS LOCATED on the 12th floor of a midtown office building. You'll feel slightly naughty as you pass the security guard in the lobby, ascend the elevator and enter through a discreetly marked door. Once inside, the room is cheerful and well-lit, the radio is playing music, the walls are painted a cozy shade of peach, and a helpful salesperson is ready to offer advice.

Owner Dell Williams founded Eve's Garden in 1974 with a 2-page catalog and an ad in *Ms. Magazine* after realizing that women needed to learn more about sexuality and take greater responsibility for their sexual pleasure. Today, the store still emphasizes a safe and comfortable environment for women to shop for erotic toys and accoutrements.

In such a hidden location, walk-in traffic is virtually nonexistent. Instead, customers find their way to the shop through referrals by sex therapists, mentions in the press or by word of mouth. The clientele is varied—largely local businesswomen and European tourists—and shoppers range in age from twenties to sixties. Until recently, men were discouraged from coming to the store except during certain hours, but Williams now says, with a twinkle, they're welcome to shop "as long as they behave themselves." In fact, the latest Eve's Garden catalog includes a section devoted to men, called Adam's Corner.

One of Williams' first products—the Magic Wand vibrator that was made famous by an endorsement from sex therapist Betty Dodson—is still a bestseller.

The usual range of dildos and plugs, vibrators, massage oils, lubricants, and S/M accessories is also available in a wide price range.

What we like best about Eve's Garden is that there are sample or demo items of almost everything in stock, including vibrators. You can also sample honey dust and sensual massage oils. The approachable salespeople answer questions about the items for sale in a straightforward and tactful way, and can put even the shyest of customers at ease.

There's also a nice assortment of books and videos, both erotic and instructional, for hetero and gay customers. After all, says Williams, "My purpose is not only to titillate, but educate." —*JG*

Fantasy Party

333 6th Avenue between West 3rd and West 4th Streets
646-230-0407

24 hours a day, 7 days a week
www.fantasyparty-x.com

FANTASY PARTY, WITH ITS IMMENSE, YELLOW, CARnival-like sign, is tough to miss. The shop is directly across the street from the famous West 4th Street basketball courts, which features top-notch hoops, especially in the summer. Being in such close proximity to a bunch of muscular, sweaty guys who are slamming and jamming has got to be good for business.

Hanan, one of the managers, confides to us that most of the store's products are designed for women. We saunter by an impressive collection of sexy high-heeled footwear—from pouty pinks to drop-dead reds. Hanan then escorts me to the "over 18" section of the store, a triangular-shaped room filled with dildos, clit stimulators,

Condomania

I F RALPH NADER WERE TO TRY HIS HAND AT THE retail condom business, the result might be something like Condomania. This is a store that is well conceived and consumer friendly. First, there is the packaging. Many of the condoms come singly wrapped so you can try different styles on for size (not right in the store, mind you). No need to be saddled with a pack of ill-fitting magnums or little guys—and neither you nor your duvet will require a trip to the cleaners.

Condoms of every description cover an entire wall and are displayed with helpful and informative "reviews". A team of researchers a la Consumer Reports has been hard at work road testing each variation on a theme. And variations there are many, including the innovative Reality condom, designed to be worn by women.

There are those who may feel that condoms suck, but never let it be said that Condomania exists in a vacuum. This is an outlet that won't let these difficult times put you off your performance. Embrace your loved one in a fit of patriotic passion by donning the red, white, and blue and bask in the glow of knowing that the proceeds for these tri-color ticklers are donated to the Red Cross. Does your partner have a thing for men in uniform? No need to feel naked as the PDNY T-shirt gets ripped off so long as Peter pecker is snugly tucked into a cop condom. Condomania doesn't restrict itself to prophylactic paraphernalia. If your flag is at half-mast, assistance is at hand. There are books, accessories, and even safer-sex workshops to see you through both hard times and soft. —*SS*

351 Bleecker Street between Charles and West 10th Streets
212-691-9442
Su-Th: 11am-11pm; F-Sa: 11am-midnight
www.condomania.com

XXX DVDs, penis pumps, and a selection of very lifelike cocks in a variety of sizes and colors. His best selling item is the Jack Rabbit, a vibrating dildo that was featured on an episode of *Sex and the City*. This little dynamo has a set of rotating beads midway under the head to stimulate the vagina and a set of rabbit ears that massages the clit. Double your pleasure, double your fun.

Should you be interested in flaunting your sexuality while simultaneously demonstrating your New York pride, Fantasy Party stocks leather paddles, whips, and men's bikinis—all emblazoned with the NYPD logo. There are gag gifts galore here, many of which make for great party favors. I was drawn to the wind-up Whackin' Willy, a replica of William Jefferson Clinton, with his oft-discussed third leg in full view. The penis-shaped cookies and chocolate lollipops would probably liven up your next dinner party, and since we're on the subject of penises, try using the penis-shaped water bottle the next time you're trying to get a rise out of your opponent on the tennis court.

Alon, the shop's other manager, points out that the massage lotions and gels are all big sellers, especially the red passion fruit by Wet. Hanan recommends trying the lickable cinnamon body gel, which generates instant warmth when applied. He's also pretty keen on the Love Swing, but make sure, he cautions, that it's firmly anchored to the ceiling. "I tried it. It's very good," he adds with a sheepish grin. —DD

London Boutique
85 Christopher Street near 7th Avenue South
212-647-9106
Su-Th: 10am-midnight; F-Sa: 10am-2am

WALKING INTO THIS GLITZY, COLORFUL, AND HAPPY shop was a fun and eye-opening experience. Richard, the manager, and Ben, a sales associate, were quite open and

congenial. "Ask us any questions about S/M, gay, lesbian...anything," Ben offered.

London is an adult novelty shop featuring such amusing, frivolous fare as gummy penises and boobs ($4.99/box), Dirty Minds and Special Secret—erotic games, edible undies in shades of pink champagne, cherry, and chocolate ($7.99)—for both men and women, and X-rated fortune cookies. All of the above are ideal for bachelor and bacherlorette parties.

Richard and Ben proudly showed off their DVD and video section, which, they proclaimed, includes the "best of the best" porn producers. Vids by Andrew Blake, Candida Royalle, Privates, Vivid, and Wicked Productions sit alongside S/M, gay, lesbian, bisexual, and transsexual porn.

The shop's best-selling vibrator is the rotating rabbit with pearls ($24.99)—a well-known tickler that flies off the shelves as soon as a new shipment arrives. Alongside the rabbit were the Small Probe ($10.99) and the scary Triple Ripple Butt Plug ($16.99). Lube is a big seller here, with Eros and Astro Glide being the customer favorites.

Both Richard and Ben leaned in close as they confided in me that they outfit some of the most famous strippers and drag queens in town. Indeed, I found 6-inch patent leather stilettos in size 14M, as well as a range of accessories from Frederick's of Hollywood, Sunset Strip, and Femme Fetiche. Going to a costume party or just interested in acting out a scene at home? Consider the princess warrior get-up ($74.99) or a chambermaid's outfit ($69.90).

The bottom line is that London has just about any novelty that any person of any gender or persuasion could possibly desire. "All human beings want different things. You understand!" Richard admonished.   —*SES*

> If God had intended us not
> to masturbate, He would have
> made our arms shorter.
>
> —George Carlin

Naughty & Nice

212 West 80th Street between Broadway
and Amsterdam Avenues
212-787-1212
M, Th, F: 11 am-7:45 pm; Tu-W: 11 am-7 pm;
Sa: 11 am-9 pm; Su: noon-5pm
Private appointments available

Only a stone's throw from Zabar's and the chic boutiques of the Upper West Side, Naughty & Nice offers a comfortable atmosphere in which to explore and experiment with the latest sex toys. The three rooms offer a wide variety of merchandise including, lingerie, costumes, leather harnesses, velvet hooded capes, high heel boots, oils and lotions, videos, vibrators, erection cream, edible undies, massage kits, and cock rings. Large women take heart, Naughty & Nice carries sizes up to 4X.

The owners are the husband and wife team of Jerry and Elyse, both of whom are former sex educators. The duo's teaching and counseling experience is readily apparent as they waste little time in covering all the bases on how to safely and properly use the various gadgets and equipment. Jerry and Elyse are in the business of pleasure and their goal is to show you how to have fun while playing safe. Sure you may have fantasized about being whipped, but do you know what it really feels like? No problem. Just ask Jerry for a demo. He'll be happy to oblige. Afterwards you may decide that a spanking with a paddle is more your style.

On the third Sunday of each month, Naughty & Nice sponsors an educational workshop on a range of tantalizing topics. During my visit, the discussion focused on the world of BDSM (Bondage, Dominance, Slave, Master). The workshops are appropriate for both complete novices and veteran practitioners. Don't worry, no nudity is ever required and refreshments are served. Reservations are a must. The cost of admission—$10—can be applied to any purchase.

Naughty and Nice also offers Girls' Night Out parties for bridal showers, high school reunions, birthdays, and

MasturBakers

LOCATED WITHIN THE OLD DEVIL MOON RESTAUR-ant, Masturbakers was launched in the mid '90s as a way for the restaurateurs to make a few extra bucks during non-business hours—and they've been at it ever since. The specialty here is customized birthday, anniversary, wedding, Valentine's Day, and hen's-party cakes—in angel's food and chocolate. And as the name of the establishment implies, this isn't your grandma's bakery. The emphasis is on erotic-themed treats.

MasturBakers' cake portfolio offers a range of designs, from tame (a tasty pair of boxing gloves prepared for Mike Tyson's birth-day bash) to extremely raunchy (a cake portraying a gorilla ejacu-lating while getting head from a cave woman). The cakes come in many shapes and sizes. Popular choices include penises, tits, female torsos (tits and pussy included), asses, and mouths. The "brown shower" design is said to be a current favorite.

Cakes can be dressed up in infinite ways. Impress your friends by adding a candy standup cock, a pair of panties made of icing, or inscriptions such as: To have and to hold; A hard man is good to find; and Breast Wishes. Great for parties, the cakes start at $40 a crack. To avoid a spanking, give Tami and her jolly crew at least three days notice. Get a mouthful, and make sure to swallow! —MH

511 East 12th Street between Avenues A and B
212-475-0476
M-Su: 10am-11pm
www.masturbakers.com

other special occasions. You can sip some champagne and have the knowledgeable (female) staff demonstrate sex toys, answer your questions, and suggest ideas on how to rev up your sex life.   —*KM*

Pink Pussy Cat Boutique

167 West 4th Street between 6th and 7th Avenues
212-243-0077
Daily: 10am-2am (Friday + Saturday until 3am)
www.pinkpussycat.com

THE PINK PUSSY CAT IS THE GRANDDADDY OF New York City sex shops. It's been around since the sex-crazed days of the early '70s—and is still going strong. The store itself is on the petite side, but in this case size doesn't really matter. All the toys and games are kept in glass cabinets, purposely out of reach of the customers' hot little fingers. Hundreds of dildos and other playthings beckon to be liberated from such cruel incarceration.

The selection here is quite varied—there are videos, gag gifts, leather and vinyl clothing, condoms, costumes, and more. Oddly enough, the UPS outfit is one of the top selling costumes. Hmmm, maybe those guys deliver more than just packages.

Ladies gravitate (and gyrate) to the lifelike five-speed Tongue II, which simulates oral sex; and the Vibrating Pleasure Periscope, which allows you to see yourself as only your gyno does—with a twist, of course. Place the vibrating scope inside and watch the action through the viewer window.

The Pink Pussy Cat is for everyone—from security guards on lunch hour to college kids to curious couples looking for a new kick.   —*DD*

Pleasure Chest

156 7th Avenue South between Charles
and Perry Streets
212-242-2158
M-Su: 10am-midnight
www.apleasurechest.com

THE PLEASURE CHEST STOCKS A COMPREHENSIVE
range of erotic treasures. Bridal shower or golden shower,
this is the place for your bachelor/bachelorette party
booty. The Pleasure Chest is a shrine to the versatility of
the penis, as demonstrated by the truly awesome range of
pecker tchotchkes on offer. Candles, lights, soap on a rope,
punching bags, shot glasses, water bottles—whatever your
pleasure—it's probably available in phallic form.

If it is indeed pleasure you're after, there are vibrators
for every occasion. And for the horny beast in your life,
there are prosthetic penises of elephantine proportions, as
well as many more modest offerings. And chances are
you'll get something smaller rather than larger if your
man bestows upon you a rechargeable penis. According to
Jimmy Amarante, the manager of the Pleasure Chest, it is
a rare breed of man who will purchase a vibrator boasting
larger dimensions than his own equipment, and there are
many diminutive dicks here for the picking. If, dear John,
there is no woman in your life, and this is a source of frus-
tration for you, why not purchase the Clone? The Clone is
a "life-like" vibrating vagina. Feel like a change? Don't just
stop at the left hand. Why not pick up a pussy with inter-
changeable hair. Resembling Mr. Potato Head a little in
concept and design, it affords you the opportunity to give
Mr. Potato, head.

Are you a woman that doesn't need a man to get ahead?
The Pleasure Chest also stocks dildos that aim to satisfy
rather than horrify, and the sleek, bullet-shaped model is
available in a range of colors other than pink or brown. For
those who do like the color brown perhaps the realistic
replica of Juli's ass—whoever Juli is—will fill your bag. Or

maybe the jelly anal balls are more your cup of tea. Just make sure you know what to do with them, as the instructions on the packet go no further than "wash after use." Perhaps it's best you consult the knowledgeable staff to answer the questions about sex toys that vex both girls and boys. —SS

Purple Passion
211 West 20th Street between 7th and 8th Avenues
212-807-0486
Daily: noon-7pm; Th: noon-9pm
www.purplepassion.com
ppassion1@aol.com

IT'S SOMEWHAT IRONIC THAT THIS QUIET CHELSEA BLOCK, which is the home of the NYPD's 10th precinct, is also the locale of one of the city's most popular fetish boutiques. In the space of what was once DV8, Purple Passion/DV8 is a veritable heaven on earth for those into BDSM and fetishwear. The recently renovated shop, which sports purple walls, sprawls across 4,000 square feet and includes a terrific downstairs space that is used for both art exhibits and workshops.

The sales people are friendly, respectful, knowledgeable, and attentive, but not pushy, making the store a delight for those who just like to browse. And the customers—a rather mixed group—seemed to be quite friendly as well. They were browsing the racks and chatting back and forth about size and fit as if they were at Bloomies. One shopper, a noted photographer as it turns out, even asked for my help zipping up a rubber dress she was trying on.

The selection of fetishwear is truly extensive and will likely please both the mistress and master in your life. All your favorite labels are here including Skin Two, Ectomorph, Naughty Nancy, and Polymorphe. We were especially keen on a latex nurse outfit ($300) by House of Harlot and a

chain mail hood ($289). There's also a huge assortment of leather blindfolds, whips, floggers, spiked collars, corsets, and boots. Towards the back of the shop is a freestanding steel cage, which we couldn't help but think is reserved for customers who misbehave.

Atop the display case near the front of the shop sits a Purple Passion Barbie—no joke. Her original outfit—a conservative purple chiffon number—has been replaced by a racy, purple leather dress. Also near the store's entrance is a solid selection of educational books and videos as well as some fascinating S/M figurines. We would be remiss if we didn't mention the hard-to-overlook dildos by Domestic Partner, a French company. If size is your thing, check out their 14-inch-long, 6-inch-wide dong that goes for $120. According to the sales person, it's a big seller. —*PG/AK/EC*

Ricky's Urban Groove

988 8th Avenue (bet. 56th & 57th Sts), 212-957-8343,
M-F: 9am-10pm; Sa: 10am-9pm; Su: 11am-8pm

44 E. 8th St. (bet. B'way & University Pl), 212-254-5247,
M-F: 9am-10pm; Sa: 10am-11pm; Su: 11am-10pm

466 6th Ave. (bet. 11th & 12th Sts), 212-924-3401,
M-Th: 8am-11pm; F-Sa: 9am-midnight; Su: 10am-11pm

718 B'way (bet. W. 4th St & Washington Pl), 212 979-5232,
M-F: 9am-10pm; Sa: 10am-11pm; Su: 10am-11pm

590 B'way (bet. Houston & Prince Sts) 212-226-5552,
M-Th: 9am-10pm; F-Sa: 9am-11pm; Su: 9am-9pm

112 W. 72nd St. (bet. B'way & Amsterdam), 212-769-3678,
M-Sa: 9am-9pm, Su: 10am-8pm

IF YOU'RE FEELING A BIT SELF-CONSCIOUS, SHY, OR embarrassed about strolling into a hardcore erotic boutique like the Pleasure Chest or the Pink Pussycat, Ricky's Urban Groove is just what the doctor ordered. Ricky's is an energized and inviting drugstore/cosmetic/novelty/costume shop. From the vinyl-clad, fish-netted, tongue-in-cheek S&M mannequins to the colorful, fun merchandise, the spirit is playful, not intimidating. Here you can find everything from traditional lip gloss to pussy lip gloss.

There are several locations throughout the city, but the best and biggest branch for the carnally inclined is the West 72nd Street flagship store. Head straight to the back of the shop for the "hot stuff". Here you'll find three areas to play in.

The Erotica 101 section boasts a full range of Kama Sutra products, as well as oils and powders, Wash Your Sins Away soaps, Virgin/Slut hand and body cream, and even a laminated card of the Tao of Sexual Positions. If you start feeling a bit peckish, pick up a box of penis-shaped pasta or "peter" butter.

Next scoot over to the Playground where dozens of pairs

Tristan Taormino

JAMES BROWN IS NO LONGER THE HARDEST WORK-
ing man in town. Tristan Taormino is a columnist for the
Village Voice, editor-at-large for *On Our Backs*, series editor of the annual Best Lesbian Erotica anthology, lecturer
and sex educator, double tee—"TT"—as she signs her emails, is
quite busy. Current projects include the second installment of her
best-selling and critically acclaimed *Tristan Taormino's Ultimate
Guide to Anal Sex*—both the book and the video—several anthologies, and a secret deal with a cable network. TT has been known to
take to the road for months at a time promoting her work.

Taormino cites Susie Bright, Patrick Califia-Rice, Annie
Sprinkle, Carol Queen, and Betty Dodson as major influences.
She says their writings and involvement with alternative sex
education and sex-positive lesbian activism have helped her
forge a career as a sexpert—an option that was not easily available to women when she was growing up in the 1980s.

Taormino graduated with honors from Wesleyan University. Her
undergraduate thesis focused on butch-femme sexual dynamics
and made substantial references to both porn and S/M. Although TT
contemplated attending law school (to continue her radical lesbian
and gay activism), her school counselor told her to write about sex
instead. And who says guidance counselors are useless?

Today, TT lives quietly in Brooklyn with Red, her lover, and
their two dogs, Reggie and Jordan. On the day of our interview,
Taormino was waiting for the plumber in the fixer-upper she and
Red bought in 2000, and she resembled any other homeowner.
But this girl is different. She maintains an open relationship and
is an equal opportunity lover. "I sleep with people of all genders.
Please do not write both genders, because there is a range."

TT is notorious for her video in which she has everyone she
knows fuck her up the ass. While it makes some people uncomfortable, her workshops based on her book and video attracts
mostly straight couples. Just a day in the life of one of New York
City's brightest and most intriguing sex stars. —*SES*

www.puckerup.com

of panties and thongs as well as a full line of Rubbawear items await your selection (we found a black corselet for $49.95 and a chain choker dress for $40). Because Ricky's has a large following among theatre-types and drag queens,

What's the Buzz?

THE WONDERS OF TECHNOLOGY ARE NOT LOST ON sexual pleasure. Whether you're a personal appliance virgin or looking to beef up the goody drawer, there's a vibrator out there for you. But how do you know which one to choose? There are shafts, wands, Swedish massagers, eggs, pearls, hands-free, remote-controlled—the choices can be overwhelming. Just take a deep breath and we'll guide you through the process.

First order of business: decide what type of stimulation you want. Many vibrators are designed for double duty, stimulating the clitoris and vagina at the same time. You can also mix and match toys, such as using a clitoral vibrator with a dildo or butt toy. When selecting a vibrator for anal, rectal and/or prostate stimulation, keep in mind that what goes in must come out. If using a straight vibrator, make sure it is long enough so that you can keep a good grip on it. (For this reason, egg vibrators are not suggested for anal use.) Several items are specially designed for anal use, such as vibrating butt plugs (widest in the middle with a tapered base) and vibrators with a "branch" perpendicular to the shaft that prevents it from going in too far to be retrieved. G-spot toys are also great for targeting the prostate. A couple of items designed exclusively for men include vibrating cockrings and sleeves that encase the penis.

Vibrators are either battery-operated or coil-operated (or plug-ins). The coil varieties offer the strongest vibes and have an average lifetime of 15-20 years, but they are also more expensive. Battery vibrators let you roam free, however their lifespan is comparatively limited.

First-time buyers need not break the bank. There are plenty of quality battery-operated models between $15 and $30, while higher-end coil vibrators will set you back about $40-$50.

The two most popular battery operated models are the Hitachi Magic Wand and Dr. Vibe. Both are marketed as general massagers, but do much more than loosen up your lower back. These are ideal

they offer an extensive collection of fantasywear, including fishnet and latex bodywear, catsuits, and red hot vinyl minis.

The XXX room is curtained off by a set of dangling whips. Once you slink under them, you'll find, among

for use with a partner. Each has a vinyl cap and can be used as is or with snap-on attachments like the G-spotter and the "hugger" or "cum cup" (a tulip shaped attachment that cups the head of the penis). Attachments run an additional $5 each.

Vibrators come in all colors, and some even glow in the dark. Waterproof models, like the Tsunami and the Lustre Vibe, can be used in the bathtub or Jacuzzi. Powerful, quiet and compact, the Wrist Rocket is perfect for stress relief in the workplace. It's not much bigger than a key chain, proving that size doesn't always matter. Your coworkers will never suspect what's going on beneath your desk. And novelty vibrators—like the Hello Kitty Vibe, which fits in your purse or the Gunslinger, which fits in your holster—make great gifts.

So many choices! Which is why it's key to try before you buy. A good shop should always allow, even encourage you, to test drive a potential purchase. Hand demonstrations only, for the obvious hygienic and social reasons, but that's enough to give you an idea of what you're taking home. Compare different styles and models. Get a feel for the varying texture, shape, size, strength, and vibe-power of your candidates. Many vibrators are designed with variable speeds to help you find the frequency that's best for you. Check out special features like clit prongs and swiveling mid-sections.

Lastly, here are a few tips to keep your new best friend humming at optimal capacity. Duracell batteries can be too strong and reduce the life of your toy so it's best to use Energizer or non-alkaline batteries. Remove batteries from vibrators when storing to prevent corrosion that could ruin the motor. Clean your toy between uses, especially if you're sharing with friends. Wash silicone vibrators with antibacterial soap after each use, but be careful not to get water inside mechanism of the toy. Non-silicone vibrators are best covered with a fresh condom during use to prevent the spread of bacteria or disease. This is also a quick alternative for silicone types.

For more info, refer to Good Vibrations by Joani Blank (Down There Press) or see the "Vibe Coach" at www.babeland.com. —SC

other goodies, a blowup doll of a police woman ($59.95), which is billed as having bulletproof nipples, but we urge you not to try and verify that claim!! You'll also encounter dildos and vibrators galore, from traditional "massage" to executive cigar, and from glow-in-the-dark to the delicate pink scallop shell model with a built-in clit stimulator. If you'd rather go deep in another direction, check out the Millennium Anal Beads, glistening with ersatz mother-of-pearl ($12.99). Sorry, but there are no in-store demos!

Since Ricky's is also a drug store, it should come as no surprise that they offer a respectable collection of condoms. Try the glow-in the dark or cola-flavored varieties.

And before you leave, pick up some candles and incense as well as a set of ChopDicks chopsticks to impress your next dinner date. —*LG*

Six Collection
597 6th Avenue between 17th and 18th Streets
212-620-3954
Daily: 10 am-5 am
www.bestporncity.com

A RECENT ADDITION TO NEW YORK'S EROTIC boutique scene, Six Collection is likely to be around for a while. The shop carries a large variety of sexy clothing including lots of vinyl. If dressing up like a fire fighter, police officer, or Wonder Woman is your thing, you're in luck—Six Collection carries all of these costumes and more. It also stocks leather garments, corsets, and bikinis for both men and women. And for fetish fans, there are lots of leather leashes, whips, and cuffs.

In the rear of the store, there's a section of men's and women's underwear, as well as some clubwear. Women's shoes come in both men's and women's sizes, so crossdressers should have no problem finding a suitable pair.

One wall of the store is dedicated to sex toys—from the popular Butterfly and Dolphin clit stimulators to a 12-inch super-cock. There are a variety of blow-up dolls as well.

And cock ring aficionados should rejoice, as Six Collection has one of the largest selections around. And of course, the standard gels, lotions, oils, and condoms are here for the picking as are both hetero and gay DVDs and videos.

The staff was rather laid back, although one salesperson did take time to show us around. During our tour we overheard one baffled customer ask, "What do you do with a butt plug?" Hmmm. We wonder.   —*DD*

Tic Tac Toe Birthday Suit

163 West 4th Street between 6th and 7th Avenues
212-206-7335
M: 11am-11pm; T-Th: 11am-midnight.; F-Sa: 11am-1am; Su: noon-11pm
www.likebirthday.com

TIC TAC TOE BIRTHDAY SUIT DOESN'T EXACTLY sound like an erotic boutique, however the store's neon-lit window—which displays a schoolgirl's "abbreviated" uniform and a slinky nurse's outfit—makes it perfectly clear what sort of merchandise lies within.

Downstairs in the split-level, tourist-mobbed shop is an array of exotic clothing and dancewear, for both men and women. Dildos, interactive erotic games, and XXX videos can also be found here. Guys in search of the perfect masturbatory toy will be delighted with a replica of porn star Kobe Tai's pussy and ass.

Upstairs features S/M and fetish paraphernalia including the standard whips and chains, leather masks, paddles, and wrist restraints. Unlike most erotic boutiques, Tic Tac Toe also stocks tasteful lingerie. Some gag gifts for bridal showers and bachelor parties sit on glass counters in the rear of the store, but seem to be an afterthought. Kama Sutra lotions and powders are in abundance here as is tantric tackle like scented oils, aromatic candles, and balms and creams that promise to prolong pleasure. We were amazed at the wide variety of pasties—colorful, sequined, and cap-shaped. Of all her tempting toys, Carla, the manager, singled out two worth giving a whirl—the Japanese Rabbit, a.k.a. Jack Rabbit, a dildo with rotating beads in the middle of the vibrating shaft made popular by HBO's *Sex and the City*, and the Pocket Rocket, a vibrator from porn star Juli Ashton's line of toys. The latter comes with a jelly sleeve that's sure to make you, um, shudder! —*DD*

Toys In Babeland

94 Rivington Street between Orchard and Ludlow Streets
Daily: noon-midnight
212-375-1701
www.babeland.com

MY FRIEND AND I WERE STANDING AT THE COUNTER of this small erotic boutique when, armed with a Fukuoko vibrator on her finger (only $25), she put her arm around me, and motioned toward my crotch. "We could be standing at a bar anywhere and I could be doing you and nobody would know." The young, multi-pierced woman at the counter laughed a hearty laugh. Her reaction pretty much sums up the spirit at Toys. This shop is all about fun, pleasure, and fantasy.

Toys In Babeland is tucked away on the Lower East Side, and makes an odd bedfellow with the cheap tailors, cut-rate men's suit retailers, drycleaners, and ethnic restaurants that surround it. Unlike most sex emporiums, Toys is fairly discreet. The storefront windows are covered with a black scrim and a large black flag bearing the shop's name in bronze along with a tasteful, rotating seasonal display, are the only indicators of what lies within.

Exploring here is a sheer delight. We pored over the erotic anthologies and sex instruction manuals, as well as the lesbian, fetish, and general sex magazines, not to mention the extensive catalog of erotic videos. Craving a more sensual experience, we spotted a small feather duster laced with "Honey Dust" ($20 from Kama Sutra) and brushed it across our throats. The powder contains real honey, and after trading a few nibbles, we agreed it was delicious. Massage oils, soaps, bath pearls, and perfumes in various scents and flavors are in abundance, just begging to make the trek home with you.

Just about every sex toy imaginable is available at Toys, along with all the attachments that in many cases can make the difference between your partner uttering a resolute "no" and a resounding "yes". The requisite Hitachi vibrator is here, of course, available alone or with various heads, nubs, ticklers and dildos. Speaking of dildos, Toys has the largest selection in town, in both senses of the word. Pick your pleasure: a three-inch purple cock or a 10-inch cyberskin penis with "balls." (Cyberskin is a silicone polymer that simulates human skin in warmth, friction, and flexibility.) Harnesses are in great supply as well, and customers are free to try them on.

S/M gear includes a riding crop or two, several varieties of floggers, a spreader bar, canes, leather masks, cuffs, collars, and clamps. As with any sex emporium, there are condoms—every type, size, and color—and the most excellent dental dams imaginable. The old days of cut condoms and Saran wrap are gone. These incredible latex rectangles of "skin" are so thin that, with a little lube on the underside, you'll never know it's not her.

If you missed out on Sex Ed in high school and college, never fear, Babeland University can help you make up those lost credits. The shop offers some scintillating, sizzling workshops such as Sex Tips for Straight Men, Sex Toys 101, G Spotting, Oral Sex Basics, Strap it On, and Anal Sex. Although, students don't get to practice what they're taught during class, the presenters are extremely knowledgeable and highly entertaining, making the workshops a great value (about $20). The classes—which are usually held on the second Sunday of each month at 8pm—can be very crowded and usually sell out early, so make sure you reserve a slot well in advance.

Originally a Seattle-based shop conceived as a comfortable, friendly place for lesbians to shop, New York's Toys in Babeland caters to both genders and all orientations. The atmosphere created by co-founder Claire

Cavanaugh and manager Dana Clark is so warm and cozy that even the most separatist of dykes will feel right at home shopping next to a hetero guy looking for the right dildo for his girlfriend to fuck him up the ass. —*SES/JH*

Vivid Video

100 Christopher Street near Bleecker Street
212-741-2970
24 hours a day, 7 days a week

THERE WAS SOMETHING ABOUT VIVID VIDEO THAT gave me the jitters. Perhaps it was the warning to underaged customers emblazoned on the shop's dull gray steel doors, or maybe it was the salesmen, who upon discovering the purpose of my visit, insisted on calling the manager to have him speak with me. Even the titles of some of the videos creeped me out: *Sex Sluts in the Tower of London* ($19.95), *Asian Dolls Uncut* ($24.95), and *Black Street Hookers* ($24.95). I felt a little better with the quasi-elegant covers of Andrew Blake's *Aroused* and *Secret Paris*.

Though owner Ron says his best sellers are gay pride memorabilia and clubwear, I got the sense that this shop was indicative of the worst part of straight culture and that it could just as easily have been located in middle America as in Greenwich Village.

Like a neighborhood 99 cents sex store, Vivid Video offers bric-a-brac such as Peppermint Peckers ($8), Dicklet's gum ($4), and big glasses with a penis for a nose (I didn't even bother getting the price on those!). Ron told me that novelties account for approximately 10-15% of his business.

The inexpensive clubwear that is Vivid Video's main business—the thigh highs, stockings, crotchless undies ($9-$35) and jockstraps ($5-$26.95)—is gaudy to say the least. In the back room, the clothing for women is reminiscent of the merchandise in those "dirty" suburban sex shops that cater to the tasteless. You'll find "hootchie mama" animal prints; fuzzy, fake, pink fur; bright red sequins, and pastel flowers in nylon, rayon, and polyester. Yuk! —*SES*

VIDEOS, DVDS, & PEEP-SHOWS

ADULT VIDEO STORES ARE OFTEN CROWDED, CRAMPED, and disorganized. They offer virtually no customer service. The selection can be hit or miss and some of the patrons are downright creepy. But putting all those negatives aside, these stores are a godsend for the horny males (most women wouldn't be caught dead in these shops!) who crave spurt-of-the-moment visual stimulation. They're especially useful for blowing off a little steam on your lunch break after suffering through a rough morning at the office.

And despite the Giuliani administration's crackdown on porn, there are still over 40 adult video stores around town that offer a staggering array of XXX videos, DVDs, CD-ROMs, magazines, and video peepshows. The latter—in their current high-tech incarnation—offer such niceties as dual monitors and split screens that can show four flicks at once. Whew, talk about sensory overload!

In order to avoid the wrath of local law enforcement, adult video stores in New York City must offer 60 percent "non-adult" merchandise, so don't be surprised if the front of a XXX video store resembles Blockbuster. The result is that you can now buy *Anal Intruder XV* for yourself and *The Lion King* for your niece in the very same store.

In this chapter, we'll take you on a tour of Gotham's XXX video stores starting in lower Manhattan and working our way north. It's probably not the type of tour you want to conduct for your out-of-town guests, but then you never know, Maybe Uncle Bernie would get a kick out of it. *—TH*

FINANCIAL DISTRICT: It's tough to get in the mood when you're in the shadow of Ground Zero, but sex has its own agenda. For horny downtowners, the video store of choice is **Cupid's** (21 Ann St. bet. Broadway & Nassau; 212-267-9760; M–F: 7am-11pm; Sa: 10am-11pm; Su: 10am-7pm; www.cupidssextoys.com). Although you won't find the arrows of love here, you will encounter a large selection of videos and DVDs, plus a number of peep booths. Gay porn is located on the second floor.

CHINATOWN: After gorging on dim sum, wander west on Canal Street to **376 Video Store** (376 Canal St. bet. West Broadway & Wooster St.; 212-431-1651; 10am-10pm), where you can digest your meal as you watch naughty flicks from one of five peep booths.

NOHO: Just north of CBGB's is the aptly named **Bowery Video** (329 Bowery bet. 2nd and 3rd Sts.; 212-529-3770; 24 hours), which has five peep booths and a modest selection of fuck flicks. After drinking yourself silly at Von and Sweet and Vicious and spying on the customers at Remote, sober up by watching a minute or two of hardcore action.

EAST VILLAGE: **Video 206** (206 E. 14th St. bet. 2nd and 3rd Aves.; 917-534-0377; open 24/7), which occupies the 2nd floor of a nondescript two-story commercial building, has the distinction of being the only smut peddler in the neighborhood. Video 206 features 16 peep booths and a solid selection of DVDs.

GREENWICH VILLAGE: Our first stop is **Westworld Video** (354 Clarkson St. near the West Side Highway; 212-229-1334; 24 hours) which features 22 peep show booths and videos for as little as 3 for $13. Just a bit further north is **Badland Video** (388 West St. at Christopher St.; 212-463-7792; 24/7), which offers a pool table and arcade machines in addition to every flavor of erotic video you can imagine. The main attractions, however, are the "buddy" booths at the back of the store. Two dollars will buy you about two minutes worth of porn and a special button in each booth allows you and a willing neighbor to peak in on each other.

When we turned the corner on our way to the gay-friendly **Christopher Street Shop** (500 Hudson St. at Christopher St.; 212-463-0657; 24/7), we faced an interesting visual paradox. A landmark plaque was juxtaposed with an "enter-at-your-own-risk" type of warning on the door, all on an unassuming windowless storefront. Once inside, you could easily mistake the place for a low-budget Blockbuster store in Hunchback, Texas, or some other small, far-flung town. The walls have that bulletin-board consistency, holding up wooden shelves filled with card-

Robin Byrd

DD ONE PART PORN STAR, ONE PART PUBLIC access cable TV impresario, and one part ruthless self-promoter, and you get the recipe that has made Robin Byrd into a fixture on the NYC erotic scene over the past 25 years. Robin caught her big break in the porn industry playing the role of Mrs. Hardwicke in the pioneering porn film *Debbie Does Dallas*. The exposure she received (and gave) in that landmark '78 skin flick led to her arrival on the then nascent public access cable TV scene, where she has built a local empire centered around *The Robin Byrd Show*, a mix of sexy gab and cheesy striptease that titillates Manhattan viewers on Time Warner's Channel 35.

If you're a loyal Byrd fan, you know that the diva will reward you every New Year's Eve by baring all of her middle-aged bod. In a new venture, Robin has brought her naughty shtick to Village Voice Radio, where she hosts an Internet radio version of her popular cable show. She also has a new CD, (she once recorded the hit "Baby, Let Me Bang Your Box") entitled *Lie Back and Get Comfortable, Robin Byrd Presents Latin Songs To Make Love To*. While we haven't heard it we're sure Robin won't be quitting her night job for a recording career. We need her out there, making the airwaves safe for smut and ads for escort services. —*AT*

board tape covers circa 1983. But look closer, friends, and you'll find a feast for those rundown Friday evenings when going out to frolic with the masses is just too much trouble. The shop sports the full collections of Falcon, Bel Ami, and other fave video lines. The scragglepuss at the counter informed us it was ten bucks to get through the metal turnstile to the live video feed and private cubbies (that's rooms, not little bears)—the joint sports two videos per evening (Nude Volleyball and Military Calisthenics were featured the night we visited). It's hard to miss the rules on the way in, plastered as big and bright as the Yahoo! sign at Houston and Lafayette. Nudity or sex in the common areas and oral sex or penetration in the cubbies are no-nos. But rules were meant to be broken, like the teeth on the few patrons who passed into the dimly-lit beyond. As porn emporiums go, the whole scene was private, quiet, and unobtrusive, registering a low score on the what-if-my-third-grade-teacher-is-here meter. But it's a great place to get your feet wet if you're new to the rent-and-run scene. Wink, wink—try it out sometime at the end of your next commute.

Walking east on Christopher Street, we arrive at **Harmony Video** (139 Christopher St. at Greenwich St.; 212-366-9059; open 24/7) a West Village fixture for 12 years, catering to customers of all sexual orientations. You'll find somewhat "mainstream" soft porn on the main level, along with a range of sex toys, penile enhancers, condoms, and lubricants—all to complement your video purchase. On the lower floor is the bulk of Harmony's hard-core collection, conveniently grouped by production company. A handful of video "preview" booths are available (note that the one person per booth rule is strictly enforced) which enable you to watch four movies simultaneously on two large color screens. Hitting a "ready" button next to the big blackened glass window on either side of the booth lifts the baffle between the glass panes (so long as your neighbor in the adjacent booth has done the same), setting up a video date of sorts. Curiously, we noticed a 2-inch gap under the window finished out with a stainless-steel trough, similar to what you would find in front of a bank teller. This was designed, no doubt, to allow peep booth neighbors to share their opinions of the previews, or perhaps a stick of gum or a breath mint. After our breath mint, we strolled north to **Extraordinary DVD Video** (148 W. 14th St. bet. 6th & 7th Aves.; 917-661-1460; M-Th, Su: 9am-1am; F-Sa: 24 hours) which has a reasonably good selection, but extraordinarily bright lighting. Alas, no peep booths here.

CHELSEA: Our first stop is **603 Video Store** (603 6th Ave. bet. 17th & 18th Sts.; 24/7), a clean, well-stocked, well-organized shop that beckons passers by with a sign on the front door that reads: "Family Movies." Funny, but I don't recall watching porn flicks with my mom and dad when I was a kid. Next up is the **Unicorn** (227C W. 22nd St. bet. 7th & 8th Aves.; 212-924-2921; Su-Th: noon-4am; F-Sa: noon-6am), where gay men will have a field day with the all-male selections. **725 Video** (725 6th Ave. nr. 24th St.; 24/7) will please the trigger happy among peep booth fans since each of its 12 booths show 126 different videos! On the next corner is the teeny **Serendib Video** (755 6th Ave. at 25th St.; 24/7).

A little further north and west, in the shadow of F.I.T.—which by the way is one of the best babe-watching spots in the city—is our fave video store: **NYC Liquidators** (158 W. 27th St. bet. 6th & 7th Aves.; M-F: 8:30am-4:45pm, Sa: 8am-3pm). The shop's name and exterior hardly prepare you for the delights within. This place is a XXX fan's fantasy come true. In the back room, which is more like an enormous warehouse you'll find thousands of adult videos at outrageously low prices. Most are only $10 and quite a few are as low as $3.98. The selection is fantastic and includes Asian flicks such as *Head Foo Young*, classics such as *Deep Throat*, and imports like *Perversitäten Parade from Germany* to name just a few. And unlike most adult video stores that are cramped and crowded, this place is airy, spacious, and hassle-free.

Penn Video II (336 8th Ave. bet. 26th & 27th Sts; 646-336-1470; M-Sa: 11am-midnight; Su: 11am-10pm) on the

other hand is about the size of a large walk-in closet. Our last stop in Chelsea is **Video & D.V.D.** (154 W. 29th St. bet. 6th & 7th Aves.; 9am-midnight), which has two peep booths and smelled faintly of urine. So if golden showers are your thing this place might turn you on.

PENN STATION AND VICINITY: New Jerseyites looking to kill some time before making the mind-numbing commute back home are in luck as this area is home to a number of porn shops. Directly across from Penn Station are **NRS Video** (414 8th Ave. bet. 30th & 31st Sts.; 212-290-0710) and its sister store **DVD Explosion** (412 8th Ave. bet. 30th & 31st Sts.; 212-629-6977); both are open 24/7. NRS boasts

Candida Royalle

FOR WELL OVER A DECADE, CANDIDA ROYALLE— A native New Yorker and current New York City resident—has distinguished herself as a director and producer of artistic and stylish, award-winning erotic videos (twelve in all thus far) aimed primarily at women and couples. After retiring from the porn industry as an actress in 1980, Ms. Royalle—a trained artist, musician, vocalist, and dancer—founded Femme Productions in 1984. In an industry historically dominated by men, Candida's films are unique; they are shot from a woman's perspective and promote positive sexual role models. Don't look for facial cum shots or gynecological close-ups here. Instead you'll find romance, tenderness, well-developed characters, professional cinematography, and appealing soundtracks. Oh yes, and there's plenty of hot sex too.

Royalle is a founding board member of Feminists for Free Expression (FFE), a not-for-profit, anticensorship organization. She is also a member of the American Association of Sex Educators, Counselors and Therapists

a large selection of European videos and new releases on DVD as well as 12 peep booths with swivel seats, while DVD Explosion offers primarily gay and bi- XXX fare along with 6 high-tech peep booths.

Penn Video (252 W. 31st St. bet. 7th & 8th Aves.; M-F: 9am–11:30pm; Sa: 10am–midnight; Su: 10am–7pm; 212-967-3804), across the street from Penn Station, efficiently crams a wide variety of XXX vids into a tiny space. A bit further uptown, we ducked into **Peepworld** (155 W. 33rd St. bet. 6th & 7th Aves.; 24/7; 212-643-8907) where a mere dollar buys 150 seconds worth of bliss at one of 22 peep booths, each of which offers 64 channels. But what really caught our eye at Peepworld was a bestiality video starring

(AASECT) and has addressed such organizations as the World Congress of Sexology, The Smithsonian Institute, and The American Psychiatric Association (APA).

Royalle points out that New York has been struggling to keep its erotically charged scene alive in the face of a hostile political climate, and she admits to being unsure as to the future of sex-related businesses in the Big Apple. She is sure, however, that sex will always prevail—whether it is underground or in full view.

You can learn more about Candida's latest projects and also order her videos and vibrators (her newest venture) at www.royalle.com. Also, keep an eye out for her forthcoming book chronicling her colorful career in sex, and her experiences with love, relationships, and men.   —*YT*

a couple of slimy eels (we'll let you guess what they were doing). After that disturbing discovery, we slithered a couple of blocks northwest into the two-story **Adult Entertainment Center** (488 8th Ave. bet. 34th & 35th St.; 24/7; 212-947-1590). The sign on the second floor—"No Hustling. No Drug Dealing. No Weapons on Premises"— prompted us to seek more hospitable environs.

Less than a block from the phallic Empire State Building are the aptly named **Empire Entertainment** (48 W. 33rd St. bet. 5th & 6th Aves.; 212-9679629; 9am-midnight) and **Empire DVD** (42 W. 33rd St. bet. 5th & 6th Aves.; 212-760-8808; 10am-2am). The latter is bright, clean, well organized, and carries a sizable collection of adult DVDs. Empire Entertainment offers adult magazines and videos, with a healthy selection of films for less than $10. On the first floor you can indulge in one of 18 quadvision peep booths; movies are rotated daily. Upstairs are three more peep booths as well as several one-on-one "live fantasy" booths. On the day I visited, five rather attractive women, ranging from 20s to early 40s, were vying for attention. A seductive Latina with a curvy figure, sensuous lips, and bedroom eyes caught my fancy. She called out to me, "Hey, handsome," with a devilish smile. I wasted no time walking over to her. She offered me a "full masturbation session" (meaning I would be entitled to climax in the privacy of my own booth—woohoo!) for $25 plus I had to pay $5 "for the machine" (a five-dollar-bill is required to raise

> The difference between
> pornography and
> erotica is lighting.
>
> —Gloria Leonard
> former porn actress

the mechanical curtain). I didn't want to negotiate too aggressively, but I did manage to knock $5 off the price. After handing my "fantasy lady" a crisp twenty, we each entered our respective booths. After inserting a fiver into the slot to the right of the opaque window, the curtain between the booths slowly ascended. Each booth was equipped with a phone. Suddenly I felt as though I were paying a conjugal visit to my woman in jail. I experimented with the phone for a bit, but verbal communication wasn't really necessary and anyway, I wanted both hands free.

My lovely Latina wasted no time fondling her ample breasts and stepping out of her red bra and panties. This was surprisingly exciting. Next she was spreading her legs, fingering herself, and asking to see my cock. She begged for me to fuck her. I unzipped my pants and began stroking my erect member, thrusting forward, pretending that there was no glass separating me from my partner. Next, my lover was on her knees licking her lips and wrapping them around my imaginary cock. She briefly turned around and shoved her pert ass toward me, then did a 180 and started playing with her clit, all the while encouraging me to come. I didn't disappoint her. As soon as my orgasm was complete, my fantasy mate wiped her hands with a paper towel, motioned for me to do the same, and quickly began dressing. I emerged from my booth and turned to thank her, but before I could get the words out, I heard her say "Hey, handsome" to her next lucky customer.

TIMES SQUARE AND VICINITY: Once the stronghold of adult entertainment in New York, this area is a mere shadow of its former self, having been decimated by the city's "Disneyfication" program. Even so, there are a few porn purveyors left, including the venerable **Show World** (669 8th Ave. at 42nd St.; 212-969-1856; 24/7), which boasts two huge floors of smut, but alas, no more live shows in the once hallowed Triple Treat Theater. All told, Show World has more than 50 video peep booths so you'll hardly ever have to wait to get your rocks off. We found DVDs for as low as $8 and a huge selection of CDs, videos, and

magazines. And Show World even has a men's room! Also on 42nd Street is **Peeporama** (121 W. 42nd St. bet. 6th & Broadway; 212-819-1039; 24/7), a rather non-descript porn palace with 10 peep booths.

Heading downtown, past the main branch of the New York Public Library, we turn east on 39th Street and poke our heads in **Manhattan Video Center** (60 W. 39th St. bet. 5th & 6th Aves.; 212-354-6890; M-Sa: 8am-midnight, Su: 10am-10pm), which features 9 video booths. A few doors

VIDEO BEST BET:
Kim's Video

HEAD TO THE 3RD FLOOR OF KIM'S VIDEO, NEW York's mecca for renting film exotica, and you'll find yourself in Quentin Tarantino's wet dream. Not only is the store chock full of everything from classic Hungarian cinema to blaxploitation films, but nestled by the checkout counter is an amply stocked adult section, most readily visible by the cutout of four female derrieres from a discarded porn video box.

Kim's boasts the most knowledgeable staff outside of an NYU Film School Film Theory class (just quiz them on the film aesthetics of classic porn if you don't believe me.) Step into the phallic aisle and you'll find an entire wall lined with gay videos; do a 180 and you'll face an entire wall lined with straight porn. Spin around and around and you'll have a true bi experience.

The adult video section is organized by star, director, and fetish. If you enjoy the work of XXX auteurs like the Dark Brothers or Seymour Butts & Shane, you'll find them here, clearly labeled. If your taste runs to porn starlets like the late Savannah, or the now legit Traci Lords, they each have slots of their own. You'll also find series like *Butt-Row* and *Up and Cummers* (the former featuring porn veterans going anal and the latter featuring new starlets going anal) and a healthy dose of classics like *Deep Throat* and *Debbie Does Dallas*. On the gay side of the aisle, you can pick from the oeuvres of Jeff Stryker or Chi Chi Larue, indulge in a Latino, military, or cop fantasy, or

down is **Famous Sports** (32 W. 39th St. bet. 5th & 6th Aves.; 212-398-6690; 11am-8:30pm), a virtual treasure trove of videos for the connoisseur of sexy wrestling, smothering, face sitting, and female body building.

Having had our fill of headlocks, we walk two blocks south and stumble upon **Vitny Video** (59 W. 37th St. bet. 5th & 6th Aves.; 212-764-4798; 24/7), a clean, bright shop with clearly marked aisles. To get to the adult videos you have to walk through silver tinsel—how fitting. Our main destination,

dip into the Euromale category and rent *The Czech is in the Male*. Incidentally, the staffer who served as my guide explained that classic porn was shot on film, not video, and boasted fuller story lines. And don't we all rent pornos for their engaging plots?

Next to the smattering of vintage porn and pre-*Deep Throat* loops, there's a sizable collection of DVDs. What you won't find much of is the truly fetishistic stuff, like shit videos (*Popo Club 2* is here, but you'll have to go elsewhere to find #1 if you want to keep up with the shit-stained saga of the sequel) and tranny porn (transsexuals and she-males). Kim's is also surprisingly light on Asian and Black straight porn, although there seems to be a ream of it on the gay side.

Adjacent to the adult aisle, you'll also find an amazingly thorough sexploitation section (sorry fellas, no penetration in these videos) featuring the work of the resurgently popular Russ Meyer and others. Videos and DVDs rent for $3.50 per night, and $5 for two nights, and there's a $10 minimum on credit cards. —*AT*

Kim's Video
6 St. Mark's Place between 2nd and 3rd Avenues
212-505-0311
www.kimsvideo.com
Daily: 10am—midnight

Other Locations:
85 Avenue A (212-529-3410)
144 Bleecker Street (212-260-1010)
350 Bleecker Street (212-675-8996)

however, is next door at **Kinematics** (61 W. 37th St. bet. 5th & 6th Aves.; 212-944-7561; M-Sa: 10am-10pm, Su: noon-6pm). Billed as "New York's Premier Fetish Emporium," it surely doesn't disappoint and we were amused by the fact that it neighbors a small bag store called Fellini's. We think Federico, wherever he is, would get a chuckle as well. Kinematics has an incredible selection of every type of kinky video and magazine you can possibly imagine, some at bargain basement prices—like the 6th, 7th, and 8th volume of the Slave Pain series for a mere $7.95 each. The videos are neatly arranged by production company so, for example, you can zoom right in on Bizarre Video's line. In the front of the store are three huge black binders chock full of info on "homegrown" enema, peeing, spanking, and trampling videos by such producers as Crystal, Beth Tyler, Nu-West, Leda, and Flag Concept. In the back of the store you'll find 6 high-tech peep booths. Feed them $5 or more and you can access advanced features like fast-forward, rewind, pause, and so on. We were about to leave when we noticed a set of metal steps in the rear lefthand corner of the shop. We followed them, and, lo and behold, arrived in a "secret" wing containing 9 more peep booths plus a decent selection of fetishwear and equipment. We especially liked the leather tops emblazoned with the NYPD logo.

Eighth Avenue is home to **Joy Video** (557 8th Ave. at 38th St.; 24/7; 212-239-0466), which boasts a strong collection of bondage, fetish, and amateur videos, including the intriguing Midwest Nymphos series;

X-Lent Video (610 8th Ave. bet. 39th & 40th Sts.; 24/7; 212-302-5962), with its impressive selection of Japanese bondage films; plus Kisma Video (630 8th Ave. bet. 40th & 41st Sts.; 212-354-1826), Euroworld (632 8th Ave. bet. 40th & 41st Sts.; 212-221-9404), and Playground (634 8th Ave. bet. 40th-41st Sts.; 212-391-9722). Kisma will hit the spot with fans of African-American, Asian, and interracial videos. It will also please the cheap fucker as it has a large number of clearance tapes at only $3.95 each. Gay porn enthusiasts

Ron Jeremy

BORN IN QUEENS, NEW YORK IN 1953, RON Jeremy Hyatt—who goes by the stage name of Ron Jeremy—has been performing in XXX movies for over two decades and is perhaps the most familiar face (and penis) in porn. Affectionately dubbed by his fans as the hedgehog—for the squat, bushy creature he resembles—Ron has appeared in over 1,600 fuck flicks and has directed over 100 more. Jeremy is well known for his lengthy equipment (8"), flexibility (he can actually perform auto-fellatio), comedic talent, and ability to cum on cue. Considered an American icon by some and, as the saying goes, adored by thousands the world over, Jeremy is the subject of a recent documentary entitled *Porn Star*.

After completing a BA degree in drama and a master's in special ed, Ron's porn career was launched in 1978 when his then-girlfriend submitted a nude photo of him to *Playgirl* for inclusion in the magazine's Boy Next Door department. The pic was published, offers from porn producers followed, and the rest is history.

If you've ever rented a porn video, there's a good chance you've seen Ron Jeremy. If not, consider checking out *Bodacious Ta Tas* (1983), *Let Me Tell Ya Bout Fat Chicks* (1987), *The Anals of History* (1992), *City Lickers* (1996), or *Ally McFeal* (2000). Jeremy has also landed bit parts in several movies such as *Killing Zoe, Detroit Rock City*, and *Boondock Saints*, and indeed, his long-term career goal was—and still is—to make it as a legitimate actor. —*TH*

flock to **Playworld** (691 8th Ave. bet. 43rd & 44th Sts.; 24/7) while their hetero counterparts will enjoy **Playpen** (693 8th Ave. bet. 43rd & 44th Sts.; 212-582-8275; open 24/7) which feature live peep show. A strip tease will set you back $20 while the masturbation show is twice the price, but also twice as nice.

A bit further north we encounter **Nilupul Video** (737 8th Ave. bet. 46th & 47th Sts.; 24/7; 212-333-4263), which in addition to having a strong amateur selection sports the only NYPD leather jockstrap in the neighborhood. A few doors uptown is **Xtreme Video**, (763 8th Ave. bet. 46th & 47th Sts.; 24/7) where an older crowd peruses a selection of vids that the staff insists are never dubbed. The peep booths could use a dowsing or two with Lysol, but on a positive note, the shop carries a large variety of kitschy toys including a foreplay dartboard as well as a wide array of naughty wrapping paper and gift bags. Continuing northward we make our way to the Senegalese-owned **Vishans Video** (216 W. 50th St. bet. 8th Ave. & B'way; 212-765-4732; 24/7), a sort of one-stop shop with a wall of sex toys and hundreds of video titles to rent or sell, 60% of which are non-adult. Adult video booths in the back cost $1 for 4 minutes.

Heading south and east through the neighborhood of Little Brazil, we grab a caipirinha, before resting our dogs at **Salaka Video** (20 W. 46th St. bet. 5th & 6th Aves.; 7am-1am weekdays, 9am-1am weekends; 212-382-2779), which is sandwiched between a sushi joint, a boot shop, and a swimwear boutique. This well-maintained store features super-modern, clean peep booths, a welcome departure from much of what one finds in adult video stores. But after all, this place is just a stone's throw from posh 5th Avenue, so what do you expect?

UPPER WEST SIDE: Finding an adult video store on the Upper West Side seems about as likely as Dan Quayle winning a spelling bee, but **Amsterdam Lingerie** (287 Amsterdam Ave. bet. 73rd & 74th Sts.; open 24/7) is no mirage. The small, well-maintained boutique does in fact

stock some lingerie, as well as fetish wear, sex toys, and games. It's the ideal place to pick up a fuck flick with your date after sipping a latte on Columbus Avenue.

Gay men on the Upper West, rejoice: **Les Hommes** (217B W. 80th St. bet. B'way & Amsterdam Ave.; 212-580-2445; M-F: 10am-2am; Sat-Sun: 10am-4am) est ici. Whether you're searching for a kiddie flick like *Garfield on the Town* ($2.95), a blockbuster like *The Birdcage*, or a majestic, cinematic, tour de force like the *Best of Colt Films Parts 5 & 6* ($34.95), Les Hommes has the goods to educate, titillate, and help you ejaculate. A solitary green door marked with the store's name makes this palace of pornography easy to miss. But once you enter, climb a flight of stairs, and penetrate the small shop, you won't be able to miss the Big Gripper Piston Pump ($38.99), the bottles of Wet Classic Lube ($24 for 8 oz.), and the display of dildos, condoms, and other nifty gadgets. While lubes and adult video sales and rentals (at $3.50 per day) remain Les Hommes' main attractions, those questing for fine literature will discover a number of erotic magazines. And if you're hard up for cash, keep in mind that Les Hommes buys used magazines, provided that the pages aren't stuck together. Also, take note of the special screening room to which $10 buys an all-day pass. Although the store prohibits sexual activity, there's always the shower at the New York Sports Club across the street.

—*AT, JAT, JH, JD, LF, MH, MO, MN, TH, VL*

STRIP CLUBS

WHILE THE ACCESSIBILITY OF XXX VIDEOS, CDS, and DVDs has led to the closing of virtually all of New York's adult movie houses, the city's strip clubs have managed to escape such a cruel fate. Despite an unfavorable political climate, these T&A establishments seem to be holding their own and, in some cases, are prospering.

So what's the appeal? Our theory is that while any Tom, Dick, or Harriet can jack off to an x-rated video in the privacy and comfort of home, this experience just doesn't compare to the excitement of watching a live, often gorgeous, dancer shed his or her clothes just a few feet in front of your face. Going to a strip show is a bit like going to the theatre. The audience plays an important role in how the evening will unfold and you never know exactly what's going to happen. You might witness a star in the making; on the other hand, you might be subjected to nothing more enticing than jiggling silicone. Whatever happens, at least you'll have a good seat.

Also, there's an undeniable appeal to being able to interact with the strippers, even if all you get out of the exchange is a vacant stare or a snide remark. And of course, for a little extra cash, you can actually have physical contact (i.e., a lap dance) with a creature, who, under normal circumstances, might not choose to get within ten feet of you.

To be sure, strip clubs aren't for everybody, but if you go with the right attitude and a little cash (nobody takes it off for free), you'll likely have a very enjoyable evening. *—TH*

Baby Doll Lounge

34 White Street at Church Street
212-226-4870
M-Th: 3pm-4am; F-Sa: 6pm-4am (occasionally closes
early on slow nights so call ahead) ♂

IF CLASSY STRIP JOINTS LIKE SCORES DON'T FLOAT
your boat, and you long for that raunchy-roadhouse-adja-
cent-to-a-truck-stop ambiance, Baby Doll Lounge is the
place to go. Don't let its Tribeca location fool you—this
club screams tenement space a la Lower East Side. Think
long, skinny trailer home.

The Baby Doll features two stages separated by a red
velvet curtain, which unfortunately has a nasty habit of
falling down. One stage is within eyeshot of the front door
and has a crudely built "fence" around it. The other is in
the back. Both are lined with smudgy mirrors and covered
in gray industrial carpeting.

Patrons show up in anything from a tux to bloodied
medical scrubs—there's no dress code—and there is never
a cover charge. Domestic beers start at $8 and the sleazy
atmosphere leans toward downright shady at times. The
men's room rivals CBGB's for the most toxic on the island.
The talent is a bit on the "booty mamma" side with plenty of variety—you'll find all ethnic and body types here.
The top dancers performing on the weekends gyrate to
everything from deep house to metal to soul hits. The girls
are friendly and chatty and, thankfully, the gold-digger
mentality and pressure to tip at all times, which is so
prevalent at other clubs, is absent here.

Believe it or not, almost all Baby Doll dancers are silicone free so your eyes are feasting on sheer natural beauty! There are no table or lap dances at this no-frills titty
mecca either. As a handy reference tool, the names of the
performers are scrawled on a black-light board in the
back. —*MH*

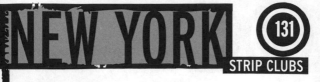
The Blue Angel

19 West 24th Street between Broadway and 6th
Avenue (at the Cutting Room)
Information: 212-252-5336; Reservations: 212-388-2988
Saturdays at 11:30pm
Admission: $20; tipping the performers is encouraged

DO YOU HAVE A HANKERING FOR STRIPTEASE, BUT
are sick and tired of looking at bored, naked women spinning around brass poles? Or are you in the mood for an evening of performance art and avant-garde posturing with a titillating twist? If the answer is yes to both, then the Blue Angel might be your ticket on a Saturday night.

Equal parts lounge act, striptease, circus sideshow, and performance art, the Blue Angel is 21st century burlesque. At times uneven, the show rarely fails to entertain the audience by mixing tits and wit to both shock and arouse. Whether you fancy exotic belly dancers, buxom sword swallowers, ex-Moscow Circus magicians, satanic rockers, or just plain scantily clad strippers, the ladies of the Blue Angel offer something for everyone. I say ladies because there were no male performers to be seen though we were told the Blue Angel is working on signing up more male acts to keep the ravenous ladies of the audience satiated.

When you arrive at the Cutting Room—one of the many generic, trendy bar/clubs in the Flatiron District—you'll have to cut your way through the dense crowd of wannabe J. Crew models to get to the Blue Angel's digs in a semi-private room at the back. Be sure to make a reservation so you're assured a table seat with a good view of the stage, otherwise you'll either get stuck up in the front behind a column, which will block most of your view, or you'll be shoved in the back where it's difficult to see over the heads of the other patrons (the space isn't raked and the stage isn't elevated quite enough).

When you're comfortably nestled in your seat, with your eyes glued to the mistress of ceremonies' fishnets, you will witness a parade of acts from the sultry to the sadistic: a disrobing Statue of Liberty; a blue fan striptease set to steamy cabaret music; a hip-gyrating belly dancer; a busty woman with a rather long esophagus and a taste for swords; a fire juggler who finds the time to strip between twirls of her fiery batons; or the lead singer of an all female Satanic rock band, who manages to find some interesting places to whet the edge of her prop knife.

And if you're adventurous enough, you might just become part of the show...by getting flogged in the closing number, or whatever the erotic fetish du jour happens to be. —*AT*

Cardio Strip at Crunch

623 Broadway between Bleecker and Houston Streets
212-420-0507
Th: 6pm-7pm (schedule subject to change)

144 West 38th Street between Broadway and Seventh Avenue
212-869-7788
Tu: 7:30pm-8:30pm (schedule subject to change)
Class is free with gym membership; day pass for non-members is $22
www.crunch.com

HEAVING BREASTS, SCANT clothing, pulsating music, sexual tension and a lot of steam and sweat. No, this isn't the set of a B movie; it's the aerobics studio at Crunch during a Cardio Strip class. The day we visited, the instructor, a guy clad in see-through pants and a thong, enticed us to seduce each other. Before you knew it we were licking our lips, thrusting our hips, and acting like temptresses.

Who knew gym class could be so sexy? Bored with the five-day-a-week Power Sculpt routine, I signed up for the devilish Cardio Strip. For sixty minutes we were taught the not-so-subtle-art of strutting our stuff, flipping our hair, and unleashing our animal instincts. We dirty danced with each other, putting our new moves into action as the instructor gyrated around us all. My favorite exercise involved crawling around the floor emulating a tiger's sensual moves.

All class members were female except for one short man hoping to get some action. The sexiest Cardio Stripper was not the fittest, but she had confidence and the right attitude. A cool demeanor is a necessity for stripping, as you don't want to look embarrassed or awkward. Dimming the lights helps. The voyeurs at the door were fascinated by our moves and couldn't stop gawking, perhaps hopeful that an invitation to a lap dance would be forthcoming. Oh, you don't take all your clothes off in this class; for the full monty, you'll need to visit Crunch in L.A.

Despite its intensity, Cardio Strip was not aerobically challenging, but most participants had a pinkish glow by the end. If you go, be sure your underwear is presenta-

ble, as the instructor calls for frequent displays of thong and cleavage. Wear that brassiere you bought for your last intimate encounter—it will put you in the mood for seduction, even if it's only for yourself!

I now understand why private strip shows are all the rage amongst celebrity couples. You may never get to perform for big bucks, but Cardio Strip is certainly a fun and non-threatening way to learn the basic striptease moves.   —*RA*

Carousel Café
75 Clarkson Street by the West Side Highway
212-627-9404   ♂
Daily: noon-2am
$10 cover, 1 drink minimum (no alcohol served)

THIS INNOCENTLY NAMED, DISCREETLY LOCATED VENue offers one of the city's few surviving all-nude stage shows and is probably the only strip club that can boast direct assistance to the World Trade Center relief effort. In the two weeks following September 11th, none other than the Salvation Army came twice a day to raid the club's ice machine so that they could provide cold drinks for friends and relatives of the victims at the nearby Armory and for the rescue workers laboring in extreme heat at the smoldering site.

When the club reopened a week after the attacks, many of the girls found it transformed, "like a Wild West bar," with exhausted workers crowding in for free drinks, eager to talk with each other and the girls. "With ambulances and fire trucks roaring past just outside the door, everything that was burning, it was hard for me to start working again," said dancer Britney, "but then I realized that we all needed comfort and escape. I started to feel a little like a USO girl." Dancers described how after completing a table dance, they would find evidence on their skin and clothes of the ubiquitous white dust that coated all of lower Manhattan. They also heard tales of horror and humor from survivors and rescue workers alike.

The club is now back to business as usual. A small, central stage ringed with tables and chairs—and strategically designed to allow a full view for anyone sitting ringside—is equipped with two poles and plays host to a wide variety of girls of all races and approaches (from innocent to downright outrageous). Performances last two or three songs. The dancers are clearly skilled and experienced; they work, and work hard, for tips only. The little they wear comes off quickly. There's plenty of pole acrobatics, shaking, and stroking (including a truly fantastic inside-out anus trick). The subdued audience seems to prefer to deliver their tips on the dance floor rather than into the girls' waiting body parts. This is an all-nude club, but despite the antics, it's far from nasty; more of an "upscale gentleman's lounge" atmosphere prevails. Table dances, apparently a little racier, can be had in the backroom for $20, and two VIP rooms are also available.

Carousel Cafe's location ensures a good degree of anonymity, and its proximity to Wall Street makes it a favorite for discreet financial types (although business at the club has apparently been slower now that the mood on the Street is less bullish). If watching the show has you hungry for a little something more, a sex shop (not affiliated) is conveniently located next door. —*SCCC*

Flash Dancers
1674 Broadway between 52nd and 53rd Streets
212-315-5107
Daily: noon-4am
Admission: $20 after 10pm, $10 before 10pm; ♂
tipping the performers is encouraged
www.flashdancersnyc.com

JUST A STONE'S THROW FROM *THE LATE SHOW with David Letterman* studios, Flash Dancers seems almost a relic of the pre-Giuliani Times Square era, back when a lap dance (or more) was much easier to come by around these parts. The red neon sign, casino-red carpeting, disco balls, faux-marble bar, and barrel-chested bouncers in

Reservoir Dog's suits all add the sort of vintage sleaze-glamour one expects in a classic strip joint.

When it comes to girls, Flash Dancers provides mega-bang for your buck in sheer stripper volume: the club's ever-changing roster of va-va-voom girl-flesh means you will definitely find plenty of eye candy. Weekends tend to have a higher ratio of well-toned Cali-style blondes sporting prominent implants and well-tended fake tans (always impressive in the dead of a New York City winter). For more spice, however, you might prefer weeknights, when the women come in all manner of New York shapes and sizes, from lean to voluptuous, with greater ethnic variety—and as an added weeknight bonus, you're more likely to spot a pair of real tits.

No matter what night you hit the club, there will

Broadway Bares

BROADWAY BARES (BB), ONE OF NEW YORK'S sexiest and most successful charity events, began as a strip show in a Chelsea bar in 1991. Conceived and directed by a chorus boy named Jerry Mitchell (who, at the time, was dancing and showing his firm ass in The Will Rogers Follies), BB has grown into an annual spectacle that packs a sold-out crowd into the historic Roseland Ballroom. Mr. Mitchell has gone on to win several Tony awards for his brilliant choreography and direction of smash Broadway shows, however, it's clear that that same creative energy is channeled into this stunning event.

As the most popular fundraiser for Broadway Cares/Equity Fights Aids, BB is one of the best entertainment values in town. The show serves up The Great White Way's finest dancing T&A (male and female) without distracting storylines or shtick. This is Broadway served "hot" by its talented gypsies who are occasionally joined in surprise appearances by mega-stars like Bebe Neuwirth, Alan Cumming, or Betty Buckley. The sets may not be as polished as the productions from which they're taken, but as it's the skin you're really paying for, who cares?

Mitchell constantly strives to outdo himself and, so far, he hasn't disappointed. He's taken the show from a random pres-

always be several girls on stage languidly stripping down to their politically correct G-strings. Still, "lap dance emporium" seems a more accurate description of this place than "strip club." Stripping, here, is secondary to the action out on the floor, and once you're seated, it'll likely be moments before some lovely lady offers you a lap dance. If you accept, you'll be ushered into one of the shadowed back banquettes, presumably for "privacy," although it isn't unusual to see patrons getting a dance at the bar, at a front table, in fact all over the place, since those back banquettes fill up quickly. The girls here are generally sweet and hustle-free in their approach. A lap dance will set you back $20 a pop; private sessions in the VIP room go for $350 an hour.

entation of Broadway musical favorites to an elaborate thematic production, which is usually pegged to some timely topic or trend. The 2001 show, perhaps too predictably, paid homage to Kubrick's *2001: A Space Odyssey*, but nobody seemed to mind the obvious. The skimpy, glittery costumes were soon tossed aside as the show took the leering crowd on a wacky erotic voyage—complete with Mylar spaceships—across the heavens.

Broadway Bares is a night of flirtatious fun and foreplay that's sexy enough for a date, but you'd probably feel just as comfortable taking your mom. There are various ticket options, but take our advice and buy a general admission seat, arrive early, and get a good spot to ogle the hotties on stage. Among the spectators are adorable chorus boys and girls who didn't make the final BB cut, and they're always looking for their next gig. Don't fail to chat them up at intermission; who knows, you might end the night with a private show at your apartment. —*TR*

212-840-0770 ext. 272
www.bcefa.org
info@bcefa.org
(The 2002 edition will take place on Sunday, June 16 at the Roseland Ballroom, 239 West 52nd Street between 8th Avenue and Broadway. General admission tickets are $35-$45.)

For early birds, there's a complimentary buffet at noon, and another at five. Drinks are the usual pricey, watered-down affairs, but the luscious topless women behind the bar will help you forget that you just paid eight dollars for that Bud. The clientele at Flash Dancers is varied, corporate suits mixing seamlessly with bridge and tunnel guys, adventurous couples, frat boys, single men, and plenty of flesh-seeking tourists on the weekends; no one seems out of place here. In fact, several years ago the club was featured in a Letterman comedy bit entitled "Can guy in a bear suit get into a strip club?"—and yep, the guy in the bear suit did indeed get into the club.

All told, the place feels very comfortable, exuding a satisfying old-school vibe. It's not too executive-swank, not too divey, with plenty of friendly, high-quality T&A to make just about everyone happy. As Goldilocks might say—if she'd ever wandered into this New York City strip club—something about the joint feels just right.   —SL

Gaiety Theatre

201 West 46th Street between Broadway
and Seventh Avenue
212-221-8868
Daily show times: 1:30pm, 3:30pm, 6:00pm;
8:30pm, 10:30pm
Admission: Su-Th: $15; F-Sa: $17

THIS GAY MALE STRIP JOINT IN TIMES SQUARE hearkens back to a time when closeted businessmen needed a place to slip off their wedding rings and walk on the wild side—or at least watch some action from the orchestra pit. As you stroll through the long, narrow space with drab gray walls—which converge on a stage draped in silver streamers—you get the distinct feeling that you've been miniaturized and transported into an air conditioning duct.

The mostly cheesy sound track is occasionally punctuated by a refreshing burst of Björk or the Cranberries, and the loudspeakers hum every time the stage lights come up. A disembodied voice introduces each stripper by his first name; the performer then takes the stage, removes his shirt, reveals some ass, and walks off. For the next two minutes you stare at an empty stage until the same guy reemerges, now fully naked and sporting a raging hard-on. He dances as the erection fades, then takes his bow (often blowing the audience a kiss) and exits.

You can't touch the dancers, but a dollar at the edge of the stage will get you some extra attention. And forget about fun costumes; it's all jeans, jerseys, running suits, and sweats. But the dancers do offer a nice array of body types and range in age from barely legal to about 25. All the boys we saw were lily white except for one light-skinned Latino. They were also uniformly smooth, including pits and pubes, when a hint of happy trail now and then would have been more than welcome.

No sexual activity is allowed anywhere in the theatre, and video cameras monitor the premises to make sure nothing goes on. There's a lounge where you can buy a soda (when the vending machine isn't broken), play *South Park* pinball, or watch wrestling videos and chat up the dancers after they've finished their routines. We saw numbers being exchanged and have no doubt that dancers go home with patrons, but we suspect it makes for an expensive date. —*JS/MHB*

Hooters

211 West 56th Street between Broadway
and 7th Avenue
212-581-5656
M-Th: 11am-midnight; F-Sa: 11am-1am; Su: noon-10pm
www.hooters.com

THE PROBLEM WITH HOOTERS CAN BE SUMMED up in one well-worn phrase: "Where's the beef?" The ogle-the-boobs-and-tushy aesthetic of this Florida transplant doesn't translate well to New York City, where there are places with both better food and better titillation—in abundance. Perhaps the most interesting thing to do while waiting for the chef to deep-fry your order is guess where all the tourists at the other tables are from—because, we assure you, few Gotham natives would be caught dead in a place like this.

We don't know if the indigestion we experienced was from the greasy food or the screaming loud orange hot pants the girls are required to wear, but, either way, Hooters gave us that not-so-fresh feeling. The waitresses themselves seemed to be drawn from the shallow end of the talent pool. After all, why work at Hooters if you can make so much more money working at even a low-end strip club—and why eat there if you can go to a real restaurant? Hooters may be a big deal in, say, Buffalo, but in New York it just doesn't cut the mustard. —*TT*

Hunkmania

248 West 14th Street between 7th and 8th Avenues
800-800-6067
F-Sa: 7:30pm-11:30pm ♀
Admission: Friday $20; Saturday $25
(advance purchase recommended; additional $5 charge at door)
www.hunkmania.com

JONESING FOR A CLASSIC GIRLS' NIGHT OUT? LOOK no further than Hunkmania, self-proclaimed "pure excitement for ladies." This all-male revue—for ladies only—features hard bodies and bulging G-strings, making it the ideal place for embarrassing the bride-to-be or titillating the birthday girl. At Hunkmania, all you need for a good time is a fistful of dollar bills and three little words: Take it off!

There are few boundaries at Hunkmania so don't go expecting just to watch. The staff is very hands on. From

the waiters to the massage guys to the strippers themselves, these hunks do their best to entice all the ladies to get involved. You won't get the full monty here as New York State law and house rules require the boys to, ahem, keep their hats on, but then again at least you'll get to leave a little (or big) something to your imagination.

The venue's layout facilitates intimacy and crowd participation. The show takes place in an open room with club lighting and iridescent brick walls. Two-tiered velvet-covered benches line the walls and a few low tables dot the periphery of the floor, which is also the stage. Twenty dollars will buy you or a lady friend a "hot seat" on stage and the honor (or horror) of being physically made part of a dancer's routine.

Performance numbers showcasing the lip-syncing and acrobatic skills of the strippers are interspersed with free-for-all periods when dancers and massage guys circulate through the audience to cater to individual needs.

They may be easy, but the hunks are certainly not cheap dates. Between the cover charge, the coat check, $7 well drinks, $5 massages, $20 hot seats, and endless tipping, by closing time you may find that you don't have enough cash left to catch a cab back home. As a consolation, if you happen to win the raffle or the fake orgasm contest, you'll get treated to a "hot body shot" (a shot of alcohol administered by one of the Hunks) or to a photo op with your favorite Hunk.

What's truly shocking at Hunkmania is the state of the bathrooms. For a venue that packs in 200 women, they have just two toilets, neither with a working sink or functional door lock. It's probably best not to think too much about all those unwashed hands commingling with the chest grease of the Hunks, but it wouldn't hurt to pack some hand sanitizer in your purse for peace of mind.

If you'd like to enjoy the services of a Hunk at home, consider Hunkmania's Hunks-To-Go service ($240 buys you the services of a private dancer). Britney Spears claims it was her best birthday gift ever! In addition to the standard weekend shows, Hunkmania also offers private parties for groups of 30 or more. —*SC*

EROTIC

Hunk-O-Mania

240 West 52nd Street between Broadway
& 8th Avenue (at Float)
866-USA-HUNK
F-Sa: 8pm (doors open at 7:30pm); private parties available
Admission: Friday $20; Saturday $25
(advance purchase recommended)
www.hunk-o-mania.com

♀

OKAY GALS, IF YOU'RE LOOKING TO GET REAL
close to some primo gyrating male specimens with bulging
muscles, you'll want to check out Hunk-O-Mania at Float.
This mid-sized club, which features an all-male revue for
women only, boasts that its male dancers are a cut above the
rest, and we certainly have to concur. Six-pack abs, oiled
bodies, and flowing hair are standard, and you'll see more
pelvic thrusts than you can shake a Manolo at. On the night
we attended, five hot performers took to the stage, each
shaking and gyrating to an adoring crowd. Every so often,
the dancers venture out into the audience to commune with
their fans and collect tips in their G-string bikinis so if you're
inclined to inspect the goods close-up, go right ahead.

The club is in full swing by midnight, filled with
throngs of excited (and tipsy) women and, not surprisingly, lusting bachelorettes. Oh, baby, Hunk-O-Mania is a
tremendously popular spot for bachelorette parties, so
don't be surprised to find more than a few brides-to-be—
and their entourages—getting raunchy and sweaty with
some greased-up hunks. For a more intimate encounter,
track down one of the "massage guys", who, said an
employee we spoke with, will cater to your every need
(within reason, that is!); or retire to one of two V.I.P.
rooms to get a little extra attention.

All in all, most of what transpires here is relatively tasteful, and the usual tackiness that one encounters at most
strip clubs featuring female performers is all but non-exis-
tent. Most importantly, every woman in the joint had a big
smile on her face by the end of the evening. —KD/FS

Lace

725 7th Avenue between 48th and 49th Streets
212-840-9139
M-Sa: noon-4am; Su: 7pm-4am
Free with one drink minimum until 8pm,
$10 thereafter

♂

TIMES SQUARE'S '90S FACELIFT BANISHED A CLUS-
ter of seedy triple-X strip joints, but this relatively new topless lounge could be the poster child for the clean, good-
natured amusement that now fills the void. Sandwiched
between a movie screening facility and a tangle of nondescript delis smack under the neon glare, this "Gentleman's
Cabaret" offers polite, arms-length entertainment, the kind
of place where a handshake is the inevitable prelude to the
$20, one-song (3-minute), lap dance.

The main room is a cozy lounge with a small stage at
either end. Pairs of dancers—one on each stage simultaneously—hold the limelight for two consecutive songs in
meticulously synchronized rotation. One of the stages has a
pole, but upside-down acrobatics would be overkill in these
cozy, mellow surroundings. As with any strip club, Lace's
sixty or so performers—who sport a beguiling variety of
hair color, ethnicities, and curves, and who work exclusively
for tips—are selling a shadowy erotic fantasy as they shed
their flimsy dresses in voluptuous gyrations to Top-40 tunes.

According to management, Lace's popularity rarely
dwindles. Weekdays draw a local/business crowd that
peaks around six and ten in the evening while weekends
are rife with bachelor parties. For reasons management
was unwilling to explain, women must be at all times
accompanied by a male companion.

Lace's champagne lounge/VIP room offers a more intimate alternative to the main lounge. The purchase of a bottle of champagne ($195 to $395) gives patrons fifty minutes in an upstairs room with the performer of his or their
choice (couples can choose this option, too), not including
tip, for a private lap or table dance. Standard rules apply

here—no groping the entertainers; no roughhousing—and the bouncers look like they mean business. —*JAT*

New York Dolls

59 Murray Street between Church Street and West Broadway
212-227-6912
M-Sa: noon-4am; Su: 8pm-4am
Admission: $10 cover plus a one drink minimum
(no charge to sit at the bar in front)

♂

JUST NORTH OF THE FINANCIAL DISTRICT AND WEST of City Hall, the suits—brokers, lawyers, judges, and politicians—congregate and relax at this venerable strip club, which has occupied the same location for over fifteen years. Friendly peelers of all flavors (blondes, redheads, brunettes, Asian, African American, and Hispanic) don evening gowns and heels to entice the drinkers who lounge at the bar near the club's entrance, generally watching sports and talking shop. Those who wander toward the back of the establishment can feast their eyes on athletes of a different sort.

In the mirrored back room, the leggy and toned dancers strip down to barely-there thongs on the two miniscule corner stages. Table dances are available for patrons who want more personal attention. Illuminated by neon lighting, the performers bump and grind to dance music and do their best to keep the attention of the audience. Big spenders can venture into one of the Champagne rooms with the dancer of their choice.

The booze is fairly priced ($5-$7) and the management prides itself on the low-key, no-pressure environment. Patrons are encouraged to relax and have a good time, which is a welcome departure from the way many other Manhattan strip clubs operate. From time to time, nationally known headliners such as Nikki Knockers, Elisa Alps, and Plenty Up Top will perform at the club. Besides gents, couples and women are welcome. —*MU*

Paradise Club

50 West 33rd Street between 5th Ave. and Broadway
212-629-0060
M-F: 12pm-4am; Sa: 4pm-4am; Su: 6pm-midnight
Admission: Th-Sa: $20; Su-M: $15; Free M-F: from 3pm-6pm ♂
www.paradiseclubny.com

THE PARADISE CLUB HAS TWO OF THE THREE elements your archetypal heterosexual male considers essential for alpha entertainment: boobies and sports. The game-of-the-moment is projected on the wall behind a three-pole runway, so that if the girls don't turn you on, you can at least catch some athletic action. Booze, alas, is not only absent but also verboten, as this is a "full nudity" club. What this means, is that the girls pull aside their G-strings to give you a live, in-depth demo of *Our Bodies, Ourselves*. Some guys find this a turn-on; others are catapulted into a gynecologist persona.

Depending on the night, there are between twenty and thirty girls in the house. All the usual types are here: wanna-be porn stars with silicone boobs; the recent immigrant from Poland with limited English; and a few black-leather-clad San Francisco refugees. There's no lap dancing, but a slow-touch or tabletop dance will run you $20 exclusive of tip; private rooms are $250 per girl per half hour.

The girls are average looking, but what they lack in appearance, they make up for in raunch. Some, in fact, smell a bit raunchy. All the same, they're friendly and willing to talk, and it's amazing how hot even an ordinary girl can seem if she's naked and bouncing around. And the patrons, a rather motley crew, certainly seem to appreciate them. Overall, Paradise is a middling-level strip club for the city. You don't get supermodels, but then, you don't pay supermodel prices, either. —*TT*

Privilege NY

565 West 23rd Street between 10th and 11th Avenues
212-243-6888
M-F: 5pm-4am; Sa: 8pm-4am
Admission: $15 ♂
www.privilegeny.com

IF STRIPPING IS A LOST ART, IT REMAINS LOST AT Privilege NY, a so-called gentlemen's cabaret located at the northern edge of the Meatpacking District. Once, burlesque shows titillated audiences by keeping certain things concealed (you've got to respect the power of the pasty). These days, stripping usually consists of nothing more than a dancer wanly shifting her hips to a blaring Top 40 tune, and then abruptly, and with little subtlety, removing her dress. That kind of uninspired choreography is par for the course at Privilege, where dancers compete for attention with the game of the moment being shown on one of the many overhead TV monitors. Visit on the weekends to find the greatest variety of dancers—upwards of 40—wiggling their wares or chatting up the customers, but be prepared to contend with one of the many bachelor parties that call Privilege home on a Friday or Saturday night.

Privilege strives hard for diversity, offering a bevy of women from white to Latina, East Asian to African American. While you sit among Wall Streeters nursing a $10 beer or a $15 cocktail, you might be tempted to buy a lap dance ($20). That's the draw here as the dreary dances taking place on the club's two stages aren't likely to arouse you. It's the prospect of titties being dangled up close and personal that pries large bills from the mostly corporate clientele. High rollers often opt for an hour in the Privileged room, where starting at $500, you can sip champagne and enjoy 60 minutes of private steamy dancing from the girl of your choice. And gents, remember, you can look but don't touch, unless you want to get to know a guy named Bruno. —*AT*

Pussycat Lounge

96 Greenwich Street between Rector and Carlisle Streets
212-285-6100
M-F: noon-2am ♂

BEFORE YOU CAN INDULGE IN THE PLEASURES OF the Pussycat Lounge (P.L.), you must first find a way to get there. The P.L. is just a few blocks south of where the World Trade Center once stood and many of the surrounding streets are still barricaded. Parking is no picnic, so you're best off hoofing it. Assuming you can find the place, you must then overcome the eerie war-zone atmosphere that pervades this area as well as the feeling that you're really not supposed to be down there—especially not to do something as frivolous as watching women strip. On the other hand, maybe that's just what the doctor ordered, so let's press on.

After traipsing across the makeshift sidewalks, enduring the sound of jackhammers, and being temporarily blinded by the floodlights that illuminate Ground Zero, the red awning of the P.L. is a welcome sight. Once inside, you'll be greeted by another welcome sight—at least half a dozen ladies of varying ethic backgrounds in assorted stages of undress swaying to hip-hop music on a platform behind the bar.

The joint is long and narrow with mirrors running the length of the bar and the wall opposite. The standard issue black lights are in evidence, as are faux chandeliers outfitted with red light bulbs. Several American flags adorn the walls and there are a couple of TVs for those who can't tear themselves away from the game of the moment. The two dozen or so patrons we observed sitting on the barstools or leaning against the back wall were mostly blue-collar guys, just trying to unwind at the end of another long day.

There's no cover and a one-drink minimum and guess what? You get what you pay for. Most of the twenty- and thirtysomething gals looked bored and tired. Some appeared to be more concerned with eyeing themselves in the mirror and fixing their hair and makeup than with making contact with the customers.

Bianca, one of the friendlier bartenders and a five-year veteran of the club, told us that the P.L. has been around for 25 years. Its longevity is readily apparent in the rows of dusty liquor bottles behind the bar. A beer costs $6 while mixed drinks range from $7 to $9. No food is served, but on the night we visited all the patrons were treated to free pizza. Hot pizza, cold beer, and naked women—now that's a winning combination.

Although it's a bit worn around the edges, the P.L. does have its charms or should I say its charmers. One of the latter was Deane, a 20-year-old sex kitten from Haiti whose graceful and fluid movements could rival those of any gymnast. The three guys who accompanied me were all enamored with her. In fact, she managed to make us all

> Sex is one of the most wholesome, beautiful and natural experiences that money can buy.
>
> —Steve Martin

a little hot under the collar and we each shelled out quite a few dollars to compete for her attention.

But the bottom line is that the P.L. is not a "destination" club. If you're in the immediate neighborhood, by all means stop by; if not, save your cab fare. —LF

===

Scores

333 East 60th Street between 1st and 2nd Avenues
212-421-3600
Daily: 7pm-4am
Admission: $30
www.scoresshowroom.com   ♂

"MO VAUGHN, YOU JUST GOT TRADED TO THE Mets eight hours ago, what are you going to do next?" Along with a lot of other celebs, wannabe celebs, and J. Crew/Brooks Brothers-clad middle-aged white guys, the hefty first baseman decided to spend a fraction of his millions at Scores—New York's premier strip club. A very unofficial main room head count on a Thursday Night during a holiday week revealed: 100 male patrons panting, 4 female patrons drunken, 25 strippers gyrating, 20 floor hosts standing, 10 waitresses waiting (for their shot at stripping?), 5 masseuses inducing wet daydreams, and an owner making mucho moola.

If, as they say, you've got to pay to play, at Scores, where touching the merchandise is verboten, you pay dearly. Walk in the door: $30. Check your coat and bag: $5. Purchase some "Diamond Dollars" (for the $20 lap dances and massages): $60 minimum, plus a 20 percent surcharge. Hey, don't stiff the bathroom attendant either, he wipes hard for the money, so treat him right! Congratulations, you've just blown $106—each (since you probably won't go alone)—and you've yet to buy drinks ($8 to $12 a pop). Dude, that's like eight pornos, two pizzas, a 6-pack and a box of tissues! By the way, bachelor party packages are also available in case you want the

company of friends to share in your morning-after monetary misery.

That said, Scores is a highly addictive, good time, and probably the best strip club in town. And you'll certainly appreciate the fact that receipts are printed blind, without "incriminating" markers, so write off your afternoon or evening delight on your CFO's dime.

The Score girls (they like to call themselves that) spend most of the night cruising the well-dressed laps seated at either the bar or in big cushy seats on the main floor. If you indulge in a dance, expect three minutes of devotion

SAVE THE LAP DANCE FOR ME:
Strip-Club Etiquette

MAKE YOUR VISIT TO YOUR LOCAL STRIP CLUB as enjoyable as possible by following these few unwritten rules. First and most importantly, no matter how "friendly" or inviting a girl may seem, always keep your hands to yourself. Otherwise, you're looking for a slap in the face, knee to the groin, or a jab from a bouncer. And, please, don't bother asking a performer out on a date. Just because she's bared her breasts doesn't mean she wants to go home with you. She's just doing her job.

Keep in mind that the performers work primarily for tips so don't enter a club with only enough cash to take care of the cover and a drink or two. Show your appreciation for the dancers by tipping, and if you sit at the foot of the stage, you really better be tipping. The more you tip, the more attention you're likely to receive from the girls. Estimate $25 for each hour you expect to spend at the club. This should cover drinks and tips. Bring more if you want a lap or table dance.

Speaking of lap dances, always find out exactly how much a service costs before agreeing to anything. This is especially true of the VIP rooms. If you don't ask the right questions up front, you could find yourself out a lot of dough very quickly with little in return. And don't be afraid to say no thank you— politely of course. —TH

and then nada. Your consolation prize for being left high and dry and down $20 is on the main stage where three times a night or so, that one stunner you've been eyeing all night gives you, and the other horny patrons, a free, three-song strip show. There's also a pole dancer on a mini-stage for those who want to get a little closer to the gratis action. Calm down, Sparky, G-strings are the standard at Scores, so all you get to see are tight bodies and post-op boobies.

For the really big spenders, there's the President's Club and the Champagne Lounge. The lounge provides a more private setting for your festivities-du-lap, but entry is contingent upon purchase of at least one $200+ bottle of champagne. Admission to the President's Club (no, it's not named for WJC) will set you back $150, but entitles you to your choice of girls for a mere $400 an hour. One of the dancers we spoke to said that it's quite common to leave the President's Room with a phone number, and that some of the girls have even been known to return your phone call. Hmmm…or maybe she was just trying to get my $400. —*MFS*

Ten's

35 East 21st Street between Broadway
and Park Avenue South
212-254-2444
M-F: 5pm-4am; Sa: 8pm-4am; Su: 8pm-2am
Admission: $20; coat check: $3

♂

IF YOU'RE AN OUT-OF-TOWN BUSINESSMAN ON A hefty expense account, Ten's is definitely the recommended place for a little tasteful T&A. Gorgeous blondes, brunettes, and redheads in various stages of undress are tending bar, hostessing, selling cigars, and of course taking off their tops—tastefully, mind you—to a variety of classic rock and disco tunes. The décor can be described as male-fantasy modern—black tablecloths, splashes of neon, chrome, and bright lights.

For $20, plus tip, any of these gorgeous gals will be more than happy to invade your personal space and offer you an intimate show, which includes sitting on your lap while removing their top. These women are so beautiful and so good at their craft that you shouldn't be surprised at how light your wallet will feel by the time you head out the door. And if continually pulling your wallet out of your pocket has left you with a sore neck, consider getting a back rub. For $30, you can have an attractive masseuse give you some relaxing bodywork, complete with scented oils.

In contrast to the performers, the beer selection leaves much to be desired and is pricey at $8 a bottle, but if you still feel like a good, reasonably-priced beer after an evening of beautiful breasts, just take a short walk to the Old Town Bar (45 E. 18th St. bet. Broadway & Park Ave. So.; 212-529-6732) or Pete's Tavern (129 E. 18th St. at Irving Pl.; 212-473-7676). Ten's also has a long-standing reputation for excellent food—we didn't indulge but the dishes we glimpsed looked exquisite.

Although you may have spent a small fortune by the end of the night, take some comfort in knowing that your receipt will merely read "Ten's Restaurant". Such an innocuous label is unlikely to raise the eyebrows of the expense-account police at your firm, or arouse the suspicions of wives or girlfriends. —*DH*

VIP Club
20 West 20th Street between 5th and 6th Avenues
212-633-1199
M-F: 5pm-4am; Sa-Su: 8pm-4am
Admission: Free until 10pm with coupon; $10 thereafter
www.vipny.com
Proper attire required ♂

YOU CERTAINLY DON'T HAVE TO BE A **VIP** TO GAIN entrance to the VIP Club, although, considering the cost of renting a private room for an hour (roughly $225 to

$250 plus $300 to $500 or so for the dancer of your choice), it helps to have a stash of cash to burn. Prices aside, this is a pleasant, elegant gentleman's club (ladies would be comfortable here as well) featuring a bevy of ethnically diverse beauties—up to 60 performers in all on a busy evening (Thursday is the big night of the week; Monday is the slowest; and if you don't like bachelor parties stay away on Friday and Saturday).

The club, which is circular in design, is done up in grand, glitzy Italianate style—faux marble, mirrors, black lights, disco balls, and super-comfy chairs on wheels. While the décor is attractive, most eyes are focused on the main stage (complete with an American flag as a backdrop—a nice patriotic touch) where the dancers take turns strutting to disco, hard rock, and new wave. The ladies each perform for three songs; they stay clothed for the first, take off their tops for the second, and strip down to a G-string for the third. Unlike in most other clubs, these performers don't dance for tips, so don't try to stuff bills in their garters. Instead, they circulate amongst the crowd before and after their performance, seeking customers who will invite them for a $20 table dance (not a lap dance mind you—there's no bumping and grinding here) or better yet, to keep them company for an hour in one of the many cozy upstairs and downstairs private rooms. We spoke with a delightful dancer from Argentina who also has a career as a singer and percussionist. Even though we declined her offer of a table dance, she was gracious and friendly.

If you need a respite from ogling all those beautiful bods (we can't imagine why you would), you can hang out at the bar and watch the game of the night on one of the largest big-screen TVs we've ever seen, while sipping a $10 beer or $14 cocktail. Or if you're getting peckish, wander upstairs to the club's full-service restaurant (appetizers mostly $8.95 to $10.95; entrees from $14.95 to $27.95) and sushi bar (regular or hand rolls $5.95). —*TH*

S/M

DISCIPLINE. DOMINANCE. BONDAGE. SUBMISSION. Humiliation. Sounds like an average day in most of the city's Catholic high schools, but for devotees of S/M, these activities are an integral part of their sexuality. Players in the "scene"—as S/M'ers dub their lifestyle—run the gamut in terms of age, gender, and sexual orientation, and can be found in just about every profession. And, as you might expect, S/M thrives in New York.

One scene veteran we spoke with summed up this lifestyle's appeal this way: "S/M is kind of like playing cowboys and Indians." Granted, the toys and costumes may be a little different, but the notion of acting out a fantasy is the same. And don't be surprised to find that these folks are just as loving, kind, and tender as the next guy, perhaps even more so. No, S/M is not about the indiscriminate infliction of pain on an unsuspecting victim. That would be a criminal act. Rather, it is all about two people in a dominant-submissive consensual relationship based on mutual respect, trust, and sometimes even love.

If you're intrigued by S/M, but don't know where to begin, consider attending a meeting of the Eulenspiegel Society (see below), or pick up one of these texts:

- **Different Loving: The World of Sexual Dominance and Submission**. Gloria Brame, William Brame, and Jon Jacobs. Villard Books, 1996.

- **Screw the Roses, Send Me the Thorns: The Romance and Sexual Sorcery of Sadomasochism**. Phillip Miller and Molly Devon. Mystic Rose Books, 1995.

- **SM 101: A Realistic Introduction**. Jay Wiseman. Greenery Press, 1998.

- **Jay Wiseman's Erotic Bondage Handbook**. Jay Wiseman. Greenery Press, 2000. —*TH*

Alcatraz

Address available with appointment
917-256-1554
By appointment only (M-F: noon-midnight; Sa: 4pm-midnight)
$20 membership/consultation fee. Prices for sessions vary;
discounts for multi-hour and multi-girl sessions
www.alcatrazplace.com
aalcTrZ@aol.com

BEFORE YOU'RE PERMITTED TO ENTER THE DUN-
geons of Alcatraz, you must first be processed, just as the
inmates of the famous prison were. But here you get to
decide how you want to be treated—or mistreated—as the
case may be. During the initial consultation you'll complete a questionnaire that asks you to rate various punish-
ments and role-playing fantasies including whipping, hot
wax, humiliation, cross-dressing, maid training, and face
sitting. You can also check "other" and come up with your
own scenarios.

The headmistress and manager of Alcatraz—which
has been in business since 1997—is Alexandra. Her team
of mistresses—and one master—specialize in everything
from nipple torture to trampling. You can view photos of
the staff by clicking on www.alcatrazplace.com. Although
Alcatraz is popular with those who live or work in midtown, it also attracts many out-of-towners.

One of the four dungeon rooms is dedicated to cross-
dressing and is decorated almost entirely in red. Although
it is stocked with women's clothes, makeup, and wigs,
some clients opt to bring their own wardrobe and accessories. There is also a medical room, and in the back, the
Versailles and Gray rooms, which are used for bondage,
wrestling, and mummification. Photos of all the rooms
are posted on the website.

In addition to the four dungeons, you'll find a mock
bar provided for those longing to be publicly humiliated.
If you're a very bad boy, your mistress will be happy to
drag you over to a nearby commercial bar and humiliate
you some more. —DC

Arena/Blaze

Call for location
Phone: 212-447-0603
www.arenablazeproductionsnyc.com
Hours: by appointment

RUN EXCLUSIVELY BY WOMEN (NOTABLY MISTRESS Leda, a respected fixture in the S/M scene), Arena/Blaze caters to a high-profile clientele of business execs and professionals. This private dungeon is located, appropriately enough, in the shadow of New York's most dominating edifice—the Empire State building.

The individual theme rooms are luxuriously decorated, offering the eye plenty to feast upon. The Byzantine chamber, for example, features sumptuous red velvet drapery, ornate carpeting, and an altar. An impeccably reproduced and outfitted medical examination room would fool any nurse or doctor. Even the hallways offer plenty of visual stimulation—their walls are adorned with breathtaking photographs of domination and submission scenes taken by artists who are well known for their work in this genre.

Meticulous attention to detail in creating convincing fantasy settings, along with an outstanding professional staff of roughly 20 dominatrixes, is what keeps Arena/Blaze's customers coming back for more. With a typical price point of $250 an hour, it's not surprising that clients are granted a good deal of individual attention. A private consultation precedes your role-play session to ensure that your expectations are not only met, but exceeded. The staff caters to clients with a wide range of fetishes, however we were told that many customers fall into the "foot worshipper" category, so rest assured that the typical dominatrix here knows when, where, and how to put her foot down.

If you like what you see don't miss their annual Black and Blue Ball (www.theblackandblueball.com), typically held in the spring. The ball attracts huge numbers from New York's S/M and fetish

communities—all primed and pumped for a smashing good time. —FS/KD

Dyke Uniform Corps

http://members.aol.com/ducny
ducny@aol.com

ARE YOU A DYKE WITH A UNIFORM FETISH? Physically fit? Crave discipline? Relish a challenge? Want more than "don't ask, don't tell?" Serious lifestyle BDSM players with dedication, integrity, and self-knowledge have a new outlet: the Dyke Uniform Corps, or D.U.C.

Members of the D.U.C. wear real United States military and law enforcement uniforms, complete with dog tags, collars indicating rank, and custom D.U.C. sleeve insignia. These women have created a militaristic institution complete with ranking officers, codes of behavior, precise rules, and even a "Master of Arms," responsible for maintaining and preserving the D.U.C. colors. At the D.U.C., uniformed pride is front and center 365 days a year, not just the last weekend in June.

The D.U.C.'s mission statement proclaims: "The Dyke Uniform Corps is a private association of women of honor, integrity, and discipline whose mission is to share a common interest in the wearing of military and law enforcement uniforms within the S/M, leather, and fetish communities." Since April 1998, the D.U.C. has been holding events and training new recruits. Joining D.U.C. is not a commitment to take lightly. According to press rep and co-founder Correspondence Officer Butch, a new recruit can expect "a lot of learning and hard work" and must first apply by mail before beginning a personalized program that incorporates training in military courtesy, military drills, correct uniform care ("shirtsleeves must be rolled inside out with 3-inch wide cuffs ending exactly two inches above the elbows"), and S/M etiquette and safety. Candidates must "demonstrate or exemplify physical and mental fitness," complete "rigorous" physical basic training, and earn their status in the old-guard tradition by providing negotiated service to the General Officer at D.U.C. events. Such service is tailored to the individual recruit, based on her strengths, abilities, interests, and whether the recruit happens to be a BDSM top or bottom. Lest overeager applicants be misled, Correspondence Officer Butch points out that "the focus is on military lifestyle and role play. D.U.C. members may do BDSM and sex with anyone they please, but we do not do any BDSM or sex with our recruits." Sorry, Charlie. This is serious stuff, for the dedicated and disciplined lifestyle player seeking regimented and structured training.

A recruit application fee of $50 and annual dues of $25 weed out those looking for a cheap thrill. Minimum recruit service is three months, with a minimum of 20

Dungeons

THE ELEMENT OF FANTASY IS ABSOLUTELY ESSENtial to the enjoyment of any bondage and dominance session. Anyone who's tried or even contemplated tying up, suspending, or caging a lover at home knows full well the limitations posed by the typical Manhattan apartment. Of course, hotel rooms aren't much better. It's just not all that sexy being dangled from a rickety fire escape, handcuffed to the radiator, or locked in a closet that can barely fit half your wardrobe. Here's where dungeons—commercial establishments staffed primarily by professional doms—can save the day. They offer clean, private, well-equipped rooms where you can focus totally on playing out your fantasy without worrying about lack of space, inadequate toys, or whether the neighbors can hear or see you. What a bummer when the cops knock on your door because your neighbor across the street saw you stuffing your husband into a latex body bag. It really ruins all the fun. At a dungeon you won't be interrupted and you can even engage the services of a professional in-house dominatrix to show you the ropes, so to speak, or even participate in the fantasy. —TH

recruit program hours, after which the recruit becomes a member at the rank of Private. Promotion periods to ranks of Master Sergeant, Officer, and General are considered in increments of six months to two years. The formidable application queries recruit hopefuls' orientation and history in the leather scene, as well as actual military experience. Of paramount importance is the essay question, "What does wearing a uniform mean to you?" A good answer is this actual reply: "Wearing a uniform is indicative of fraternity (meaning you're a part of something close, a brotherhood for example, a community larger than yourself). It's an identity. When worn correctly by someone with the correct intent it also depicts honor, integrity, discipline, respect, loyalty, and strength."

Despite how intimidating all this sounds, Correspondence Officer Butch claims it is not difficult to gain membership, "It takes a person of integrity and discipline, that is all." D.U.C. members are diverse racially and mostly butch (members wear standard male uniforms, though exceptions can be made for promising recruits of other gender persuasions). The members we saw were all impressively physically fit, reflecting their role models—members of the active U.S. military. There are currently 12 women in the D.U.C.—five officers and seven enlisted, with no active recruits at the present time. Come on, then, isn't now your time to serve?   —BC

The Eulenspiegel Society

24 Bond Street between Lafayette Street and Bowery
212-388-7022
www.tes.org
tes@tes.org

THE EULENSPIEGEL SOCIETY (PRONOUNCED Oy-len-shpee-gull), also known as TES, is a volunteer-run nonprofit membership organization dedicated to promoting the sexual liberation of consenting adults in the S/M scene through informational and social events. TES is open to anyone with an interest in dominant and submissive fantasies and related fetishes.

With over 1,100 members and 30 years of history, TES describes itself as the oldest and largest S/M education and support group in NYC. One of the primary concerns of TES is that it provide a safe space where the Eulenspiegel Creed and Rules of Etiquette—such as treating people with consideration and respecting the privacy of others— are followed to ensure positive play experiences.

Meetings—held every Tuesday and Wednesday— address various topics like fire and wax, caning, erotic writing, sensory deprivation, and piercing. Although there is no formal dress code, some members elect to don colorful costumes for the occasion. Both singles and couples are welcome. The doors open at 7:30pm and the program—often a lecture, demonstration or slide show— begins at 8. In addition to the regularly held meetings, TES sponsors excursions to local S/M clubs. One such excursion—held specifically for novices (singles or couples)—is offered several times during the year.

TES meetings are held in an obscure theater space on Bond Street near New York University. This reviewer attended a basic-skills workshop for novices. The presenter, with enthusiastic help from veteran members, first fed us alphabet soup: SM (sadomasochist), TB (top-bottom), DS (dominant-submissive), BD (bondage-discipline), before delving into the finer points of spanking (the best toy is your hand), paddling (watch for bruising), flogging (not on the head), and leather restraints (don't cut off their circulation, but don't let them get away either).

Different types of paddles, including a hairbrush and ping-pong paddle, were on display, along with floggers, and a single tail whip, with which our guide gave us a lashing demonstration. He encouraged attendees to peruse the wares. Two men examined and tested the paddles against their palms like wine connoisseurs assessing the merits of a pinot noir. Taking a quick, sharp swipe at my own palm with a small pliable leather paddle, under the surveillance of other S/M virgins, I felt a little thrill at my own naughtiness.

After we learned the skills and techniques with which to conduct a basic "scene," our group—a mix of men and women of varying ages—was invited to participate in a Q & A session. I asked a member to comment on one particular S/M club that I planned on visiting. He stated without

Reece

AFTER BECOMING FRUSTRATED WITH THE BUREAUCracy and politics of corporate marketing, Reece put his suit and tie away and got out the chaps and boots. He spent six months researching the sex trade, and in less than a year, was named "Escort of the Year" by a leading industry website. He's developed a thriving, loyal business both here in New York and out of town. His specialty is performing the role of a leather dominant top and he, appropriately, calls his work an important type of erotic therapy. Many clients claim an almost spiritual reawakening after a session with him, but that could happen after one glimpse of his strikingly handsome face or five minutes in his commanding presence. Reece's insight into his services goes far beyond simply getting the client off and sheds new light on a mysterious, misunderstood part of sexuality.

On most days, Reece gets up around 8am and goes through his correspondence. "Clients require constant, personal attention and I am always fielding inquiries and scheduling appointments." After hitting the gym, he sees up to two clients per day at a minimum of two hours each. "Any more than that would be too wearing on me and I couldn't give the level of service that I'm known for."

Reece's specialty is to fulfill the client's fantasy of a dominant/submissive erotic trip. "I'm the dominant one," Reece explains. "They don't always know what they want, so, if they're new, I'll spend the first few minutes getting inside their heads and figuring it all out for them. So much of what I do is psychological, and whoever said that the brain is the most important sex organ was correct."

reservation that as a woman going solo, I would immediately get "hit on." I assumed he meant that literally.

A one-year TES membership ($45/single; $55/couple) includes: discounts to TES parties, workshops, and meetings; discounts to local S/M clubs and S/M-related businesses; a subscription to Prometheus, the TES quarterly magazine, with a complimentary personal ad. Members may also attend board meetings and vote for the board of directors.

Most of Reece's clients are high-level executives in managerial positions. "They are under constant stress from their jobs and they need an escape. I turn the tables for them and relieve the pressure. They also want that pressure relieved in a safe, comfortable, and, above all, discrete manner. I provide all of this for them." Most of Reece's clients seek out a dungeon experience. "They know my dungeon/playroom is clean, safe, and well-equipped. Some clients want a frat boy, hazing, jockstrap scene, and several request to see me specifically after I return from the gym when my scent is strongest. They love the way I smell and get excited from the minute they walk in."

Reece won't see just any client. "I'm very clear as to what my area of expertise is and I make sure they [the clients] understand that before they make an appointment. If I don't think I'm right for them, I'll say so. There are plenty of escorts who try to be everything to all people, but I'm not one of them. I'm happy to refer someone to another associate who might be better for them and my peers do the same for me."

So why does Reece do what he does? "I'm helping people enjoy themselves and to explore entire new dimensions of their souls. I recently had someone tell me that they had been in therapy for 5 years and made no progress. They saw me for one session and had a major breakthrough. They fired their therapist the next day. I think that says it all." —*TR*

Reece, Leather Dominant Top
In/out calls by appointment only
reece@getreece.com
www.getreece.com

The bottom line: TES members are light-hearted and friendly and not the least bit intimidating. If you're even minimally intrigued by S/M, come to a TES event. Ask some questions, learn more about the lifestyle, and then decide if you want to play. Highly recommended. —*SAL*

Excalibur

212-714-2331
Members only; address released with appointment
M-Sa: 10am-10pm (Sundays available for private parties)
www.excalibur-nyc.com
info@excalibur-nyc.com

TOWARDS THE CONCLUSION OF OUR INTERVIEW, Ms. Kayla, Excalibur's director and founder, suddenly gathered up my coat and scarf, ushered me into an empty dressing room, and shut the door behind her. I felt I had stumbled into an episode of the X-Files. The reason for her behavior? The arrival of a client. Privacy and confidentiality are strictly adhered to at Excalibur. I remained closeted until the client was led into a more secure place where his identity would be protected. Speaking of clients, Excalibur caters primarily to men (only one percent of the 700 members are women)—more specifically, to wealthy white and Asian businessmen, although black and Latino customers are on the rise.

Getting in to Excalibur is tough. First, you must have an appointment. Once you arrive, you must ring the outside buzzer to gain access. If you just waltz in without notifying the staff, the elevator won't stop at the fourth floor. That's the mistake that I made.

During my visit, the 2500-square-foot space was open and well lit, but that was very unusual. Generally the doors are closed and the lights dimmed to a crypt-like level. Amenities include a ladies room (dressing/locker room), lounge, consultation room, laundry room, bathroom/shower facility, and garden suite (with a stage for drag shows). In addition, there is a medical room (complete with dentist's chair); dog room for puppy training (with a view into the medical room); den (really a suspension room with a floor-to-ceiling wood cross in the corner), and a drag room (with vanity and chaise). And, somewhere in this facility, there are wrestling mats.

Kayla started Excalibur to create a safe, relaxed, and discreet environment that touched on both the "cerebral and physical" and expounded on "consensual realism"—a phrase she coined for Excalibur's mission statement. She employs about 20 mistresses—and a smattering of masters—from a variety of backgrounds. They range in age from early to late 20s, and are hand picked by Kayla herself.

At Excalibur, the client directs the show, but must first decide whether to be a submissive (postulants, masochists, servants, slaves); a dominant (guardians, sadists, sponsors, tops); or a cross dresser (training is offered for transsexuals and transgenders). About 20 percent of Excalibur's clients choose to be dominant, while 70 percent go the way of the submissive. Other services include classes (like Humiliation 101 & 102) and couples workshops, plus Excalibur sponsors overnight/weekend retreats, parties, and special training sessions.

"Tributes"—as Kayla refers to the fees—start at $210/hour for a dominant and $350/hour for a submissive. There's also a $20 consultation fee, which is waived if you purchase a session. —*SAL*

Hellfire Club

28 9th Avenue near 14th Street
212-647-0063
Th-Sa: Call or check the website for hours, prices, and events
hellfireclubny.com

OF ALL THE S/M AND SEX CLUBS IN NEW YORK, Hellfire is perhaps the most infamous. Aptly located in the Meatpacking District and owned and operated by a big, lovable bear of a guy named Lenny, this hardcore playground doesn't quite live up to its illustrious name, and that's a shame.

S/M Club Etiquette

I F YOU GET UP THE COURAGE TO VISIT AN S/M CLUB you'll be fine if you follow some simple rules. It's important to look the part so that a) you'll feel more comfortable and b) you don't diminish the experience for other guests. If you show up at a club in your civvies, not only will you look like a dork, you'll ruin the fantasy for everybody else. On the other hand, don't feel you need to run out and spend hundreds of dollars on a black leather or latex outfit. Black jeans and a black shirt will suffice. Once inside, behave as you would at a cocktail party. Don't gawk and never touch without permission. If you see a person you'd like to meet, consider asking the bartender for an introduction, sending them a drink, or complimenting them on their outfit or bondage technique. If you participate in a scene as a dominant it is your responsibility to look after the welfare of the submissive. The two of you should agree on a "safe" word that the submissive can utter to end a scene that's going sour. —*TH*

Being essentially a dank hole in the ground, the Hellfire certainly has the atmosphere of a dungeon. The big question is, where are all the women? On some of the nights we visited, the Hellfire seemed solely a hook-up scene between transsexuals and guys who, if they were any further into the closet, would pop out in Narnia. You may not feel comfortable bringing your own date, either—when we did, eager voyeurs kept cruising by, hoping to get invited into a "scene," or waiting for something to start so they could whip it out and get their rocks off. Going into Heaven, the back room, where full nudity is permitted, we found a ghoulish gaggle of pudgy, pale, naked men masturbating while some guy blandly whipped his girlfriend. The bare, chilly concrete floors and duct-tape-covered torture devices reeked of sleaze and desperation. The place is wholly joyless—and, because full nudity is permitted, alcohol isn't. Too bad. A stiff drink would have at least livened things up.

Note also that the Hellfire converts to Manhole, a gay S/M club, on weeknights, so be sure to check the website before venturing out. Bottom line: Hellfire is for the hard-core decadent only. Beginners would be better off taking a trip to La Nouvelle Justine or Paddles first, before descending into this particular hell. —*TT*

Jezebel's

40 Peck Slip between South and Front Streets
212-962-0109
By appointment only (M-F: 11am-6:30pm; Sa-Su and holidays: 12pm-7pm; other times by special request)
$125 for the first half hour; $60 each additional half hour; discounts for multi-hour and multi-girl sessions
www.seaportsiren.com
domjezebel@aol.com

"DOMINANCE AT GRANDMA'S" IS HOW THE OWNER, Jezebel, describes her small and homey dungeon. She says the experience for clients tends to be more cerebral than physical since the focus here is on fetishes, fantasies, and fun. And the rules are strict: no submission, binding, or gagging of the girls.

The establishment is located in a commercial/residential building across from the South Street Seaport and has been in operation since 1998. The majority of clients are businessmen from the nearby Financial District. Many drop by once a week; the truly obsessive, notes Jezebel, come in twice a week. Most come to satisfy their foot and leg fetishes, while others desire to play out elaborate fantasies complete with props and costumes. Jezebel said one client wanted to base a session on a 30-page script he had written, but eventually tossed the script and ad-libbed instead.

The dungeon features two session rooms and a bathroom with a shower. Each of the session rooms is decorated much like, well, your grandmother's living room, with comfy chairs, old-fashioned tables and lamps, and a futon sofa that pulls out into a bed. But take a peek into the dresser drawers and you'll find items grandma probably

never had much use for, such as leather restraints, whips, and paddles. One of the rooms is also equipped with a cross for vertical bondage.

Although this dungeon is small, the range of mistresses is wide. Some are petite women in their 20s, others are in their 50s. There are full-size ladies, too, and even one six-foot tall competitive wrestler. Their specialties range from foot fetishes to schoolgirl fantasies to medical scenarios. Check out www.seaportsiren.com for photos of the mistresses and more on their talents and physical attributes. —*DC*

La Nouvelle Justine

101 East 2nd Street between 1st Avenue and Avenue A
212-673-8908
Bar: Tu-Su: 6pm-close Dinner: W-Sa: 6pm-midnight
www.punishmentsquare.com/justine

IF THE MARQUIS DE SADE WERE ALIVE AND WELL he would be hanging out—literally—every night at this S/M-themed restaurant. Moved from its original location on West 23rd Street, La Nouvelle Justine is now tucked around the corner from Lucky Cheng's, so if you tire of the S/M scene inside you can go there to check out the drag queens. Justine has no sign. Look for a plain red door marked with a small sculpture of a finger held to a pair of red lips. Open this door boldly. If you are lucky, you will be greeted by a hostess in a rubber dress who will take you to your table and insult you. If you are unlucky, you will be led to the stage, strapped to the wall, and whipped.

La Nouvelle Justine is dark—very dark—lit mainly with large hanging lanterns and lots of candles, sort of like a basement apartment. The walls are covered with enormous reprints of Eric Stanton fetish drawings and smaller photos of S/M enthusiasts in their gear. Ceiling-mounted TV sets show bondage films or staff favorites—one night it was Dracula—and the bar is a glass case that holds whips and collars. The S/M shows take place in the back on a small stage. They seem to happen hourly, or whenever the mistress on duty can persuade a customer to put himself in her hands. During the week the crowd is sparse and consists mainly of regulars—they are easy to spot— with a few gawking Upper East Siders slumming it downtown. On the weekend, things heat up and this secret spot loses its anonymity; there is usually a crowd outside.

The food here is secondary to the entertainment, but you can try the Lucky Spring Rolls ($6.50) or Emperor Dumplings ($6.50) to start. The main courses run from Kung Pao Chicken ($14.95) to Pan Seared Duck Breast ($21.00). "Slaves" decked out in blue hospital scrubs refill the water glasses. This will perhaps be the nicest part of your meal. At some point the mistress on duty comes to your table to try and persuade a member of your party to join her onstage for a "session." When she leaves there will be a debate over whether the mistress is a man or a woman. This will remain undecided.

If you agree to a session, be prepared to pay. It will probably cost around $20, depending on what the mistress does, but it is a good idea to negotiate up front instead of waiting until she has you in handcuffs. Once on stage let the mistress know how you like it so that she knows how to adjust the ferocity of her strokes. This is not a hardcore S/M session. It is "soft fetish" for beginners or curious first timers.

When you have finished eating, a slave will clear your table. If you fail to order another glass of wine ($7), the waitress will lean over and hiss in your ear—DRINK! Obey. You have only been here for an hour, but you have already learned a thing or two. —HT

Lesbian Sex Mafia

212-726-3844
lsmnyc@hotmail.com
www.lesbiansexmafia.org

♀

THIS SECRET SORORITY OF LESBIAN, TRANSSEXUAL, bisexual, and heterosexual women interested in BDSM

Tempest Wrestling Club

WHO SAYS A GUY CAN'T FIGHT A GIRL? AT the Tempest Wrestling Club that's their mantra, although you'd be foolish to underestimate the strength and prowess of the beautiful temptresses you choose to spar with. If you get turned on by a demure girl getting you in a leg lock and then sitting on your face, or if you're the sort who likes to engage in a few rounds of competitive wrestling with a muscle-bound yet seductive beauty, then this is the place for you.

At the Tempest Wrestling Club you can choose light fantasy and be sensually trampled and caressed by the female wrestler of your choice; or you can take on a buff Amazon in a more competitive match. But don't be surprised if you leave the ring both aroused and bruised. Then again, you can simply choose to be a voyeur and sit back and watch two girls duke it out in a catfight. And if you're more interested in role playing a fantasy than getting trounced on the mat, Tempest has options in that department as well.

Like to wrestle in mud, or maybe lime Jell-O? Sorry, Tempest can't accommodate you on those fetishes. But for an additional fee, some of the girls are open to wrestling in oil, and you can have your session videotaped. If you do the former, there are shower facilities available so you can rinse off before limping back to the office. If you choose the latter memento, just remember not to confuse that tape with the one of your honeymoon.

Sessions last one hour or longer, depending on your stamina and the size of your wallet, since pricing starts at $250 an hour. And don't bother bringing plastic, because while you may leave the wrestling ring black and blue, the girls at Tempest know only one color that pays for their session fees—green. *—AT*

Upper 20s on the East Side
212-946-5099 (info & reservations)
By Appointment Only
Sessions start at $250/hr
www.enterthestorm.com
tempestwrestling@aol.com

play with other women recently celebrated its 20th anniversary, making it the oldest known "independent organization for women of all sexual orientations exploring woman-to-woman BDSM play."

LSM holds 101-type orientations every month to recruit new members. Being a woman doesn't guarantee membership. To be accepted, a prospective recruit must first attend a safety demo (LSM places a major emphasis on safety, consensuality, and confidentiality) and orientation. Membership dues of $25 for an individual/$35 for a couple living at the same address must be paid in advance. Membership carries advantages such as reciprocal arrangements with lesbian S/M groups in Portland, OR and Baltimore, MD and discounts at local S/M clubs, sex toy shops, and fetishwear stores.

Since BDSM is taboo—both in society at large and in the lesbian/feminist community—confidentiality at

LSM's events is necessary to protect members and attendees who might otherwise be "exposed" at home, work or elsewhere. While most events are open to the public, the organization is weak on outreach and publicity, thus interested women usually find the organization through underground channels. Major events are often attended by well-known underground erotic figures and are typically publicized in Time Out New York and various local queer publications. For the most part, however, the organization relies on a small mailing list and word-of-mouth to generate interest.

LSM welcomes newcomers, experienced players, and the simply curious. The organization sponsors regular events (American Sign Language interpretation is provided on request), workshops, demonstrations and lectures on topics such as negotiation, bondage, flogging, cutting, and piercing, and offers "play parties," often at local dungeons or S/M clubs. The latter are open to women only, who must pay an entrance fee (discounted for LSM members), and beginners can either watch while the more experienced play, or, they can try their hand at any number of "scenes" with a partner (or partners) of choice. —*SES*

L'Oeil Caché
Address available with appointment
212-989-3286/3495
loeilcache@aol.com
By appointment only (Daily: 10am-midnight)
Consultation: $50; Sessions: $220 an hour; $170 a half hour

DESPITE A CHANGE IN MANAGEMENT AND RUMORS of its impending demise, L'Oeil Caché lives on. Its renowned founder, Mistress Avalon, is still the owner, but she's handed over management duties to a longtime acquaintance—known in the scene as Knight of Halos. For him, the mission remains the same: provide members a memorable experience with discretion, elegance, sophistication, and a personal touch. Some changes are planned, however, including an improved website, and the addition of a medical room and a licensed cosmetologist.

The mood at L'Oeil Caché—which translates as "hidden eye"—is set the moment you step into the candlelit reception area. Before your eyes can adjust to the darkness, Goddess Haden or one of the other staff members will make sure you're comfortable and relaxed. First-time guests receive a 20-minute consultation during which they can tour the four dungeons, review the portfolios of the staff, and meet with one of the mistresses. L'Oeil Cache has roughly ten steady mistresses—both dominant and submissive—and a master.

The Consultation Room, which features a throne, is also used as a session room, especially for cross-dressing. (Plans call for this space to be expanded so it can be used for workshops and parties, too.) If you prefer to be tied up in chains, locked in a cage, or strapped down in a leather bondage chair, try the Blue Room. Or if you would rather be strapped to a bondage table or a cross on the wall, request the Tan Room. But if ambience is your thing, you'll love the Red Room, which features leather benches, a bondage spinning apparatus, a pulley, a sling, and a black leather sofa. No matter which room you choose, the experience here will probably leave you begging for mercy, or begging for more. Vive L'Oeil Caché!   —*DC*

The L.U.R.E.

409 West 13th Street between 9th Avenue and Washington Street
212-741-3919
Daily: 8pm-close

EVER WONDER WHAT BECAME OF THE MEDIEVAL-ists on your college campus? You know, the oddballs who sported cloaks and befeathered caps, jousted with Nerf swords, and played Dungeons and Dragons ad nauseam? Did any of them get married, or, ever even get laid? One visit to The L.U.R.E. and your questions will be answered.

As we entered the club, we immediately took in a spanking scene in which what appeared to be an inflatable doll was being set upon by a big, bearish man. As we ordered a drink, got the skinny on the name of the place (the name stands for Leather, Uniform, Rubber, Etc.), and settled into conversation, the aforementioned "doll" got down off her sado-perch, fixed her hair, and mumbled to the heavens, "whoo, what time is it?"

The "bad girl" and her "high school principal" were asked politely by the bartender to hit the back room. They weren't the only ones prosecuting a little discipline around the bar. On a stool right next to us, a lesbian, big as Gibraltar, was getting a blow job on her studded black strap-on from a sorority-chick-gone-medieval with perfect bangs and heavy mascara. They, too, were banished to the hinterlands as we took in the multiracial gay porn that flickered on the club's video monitors.

Noticing the direction of our gaze, the eager bartender dropped the name of the porn director. "He's a real genius," he told us. "He's known for the kinky stuff— hands-free coming and shit." On the monitors, gay ninja invaders were pressing themselves against the French doors of a tropical bungalow while doing the cock-in-sweatpants jitterbug. We took it all in, then moved through the dark caverns and passages to the erotic Siberia of the back room.

What with all the leather and latex gear on display, we were a little self-conscious about our "Sweaters of Westchester" attire, but as it turned out we weren't forced to step into the dim light of iniquity to see what was happening in the forbidden chamber. A woman of advanced years, bearing an uncanny resemblance to Estelle Getty, was methodically thrashing a naked man with a switch of bamboo. There we stood, immigrants from the bar, at the chamber's entrance taking it in like a bunch of English-speaking tourists watching Univision. All in all, The L.U.R.E. is a feast for the senses and a shock to the system. This S/M fetish garage doesn't keep any secrets, but it does encourage pain—in the right places. —JD/MO

Mistress "Hot Boxx" Nona

www.mistressmine.com; www.hotboxx.com

A WOMAN SPORTING A MILITARY UNIFORM THRASH-es a cop. The strobing lights of a squad car illuminate the scene. The would-be soldier then whips out a strap-on dildo to inflict further damage in what will be scene two of Mistress Nona's fantasy enactment. For her, it's the ulti-mate role reversal.

Nona is considered by some to be the meanest sadist in town. This dominatrix workaholic divides her days between holding court in her outer-borough dungeon and perfecting the HotBoxx, an innovative sex toy she conceived with an ex-partner in the mid '80s. The HotBoxx is an electronic device that can stimulate three people simultaneously. Nona officially launched the toy in 2001. All one hundred units, which she personally tested for quality control, were sold, and more are on their way.

But how did this former elementary school teacher and wife of a Jewish dentist become a professional domme, sex-toy manufacturer, S/M lecturer, and publisher of *Mistress Mine* magazine? First, she got a divorce ("he did-n't fill my oral cavity"). But it was, she says, her father's death that changed her life. After his passing, she told her-self she would simply do what she wanted to do.

And she wanted to do a lot. But because of the ram-pant spread of AIDS and STDs, Nona knew that she need-ed to find a safe way to express her sexuality. She sought out mentors to learn about the S/M scene, became a reg-ular at the original Vault, and found she couldn't get enough of being a domme.

So she "chose the hard life," one of financial instability that is constantly vulnerable to the criticisms of others. For her, S/M and B/D is the most advanced version of sex-uality—the "Picasso" of sex.

Situated just off her dining room, Nona's fully equipped dungeon features a suspension device, canes

(made by an 83-year-old British man who was caned since he was six), whips (she thinks nothing of buying a $500 whip for her birthday), and a transvestite drawer that, she says, her cat keeps getting into. She takes pride in her equipment, emphasizing its quality over what is frequently found in other S/M houses.

Many of Nona's clients stick with her for years, probably because she offers a very personal touch. She regularly chats with one of her clients before the start of their session and another takes her out to dinner before his. But, she is quick to point out that sex is reserved exclusively for her significant other.

Now in her 50s, Nona is contemplating retirement from the profession, but not the lifestyle. She laments that many old-timers like herself have moved on, but she's confident that members of the next S/M generation, like Allison, her assistant of seven years (whom Nona has mentored since meeting her in a bagel shop which carried

BDSM for Dummies

I T'S NOT LIKELY THAT YOU WOULD HAVE LEARNED many of these words when studying for the SATs, but if you want to survive and thrive in the world of BDSM, where appearance is everything, you need to speak the language of the subculture.

B/D (Bondage-Discipline): In sexual role play, the practice of using restraints (e.g., cuffs, rope) and engaging in corporal punishment, such as spanking or flogging, which incorporates mutually agreed upon elements of S/M and D/S.

BDSM (Bondage & Discipline, Dominance & Submission, Sadomasochism): Generic term that encompasses B/D, D/S, and S/M and is used to describe all areas of kink or alternate sexuality.

Bottom: The submissive person in a scene.

Dom/Dominant/Master: see D/S

Domme/Dominatrix/Mistress: see D/S

D/S (Dominant-Submissive): The consensual exchange of power in a BDSM relationship where one person relinquishes

Nona's line of penis-shaped bagels) will continue to carry the S/M torch.

"New York is a tough market," says Nona. But before she hangs up her toys for good, she plans on living out one last fantasy: she'd like to be bullwhipped in broad daylight while standing in the middle of Queens Boulevard. —SAL

The Noose

261 West 19th Street between 7th and 8th Avenues
212-807-1789
Tu-W, Sa: 11am-8pm; Th-F: 1pm-8pm; Su: 1pm-6pm

FOR NINETEEN YEARS, THE NOOSE— A SMALL, cluttered shop in Chelsea—has been a popular destination for New York's fetish community. Fetish fans come for the custom-made leather and latex clothing, for the

control to another. Either a dom/dominant (master) or domme/dominatrix (mistress) is in control of the submissive (slave) in S/M role play.
Fetish: Any inherently non-sexual object, substance, or body part that stimulates sexual desire (e.g., leather, feet, latex).
Pistachio: Code word for BDSM. See Vanilla.
Play: To engage in BDSM activities.
S/M (Sadomasochism): The practice, among consenting adults, of inflicting (or receiving) pain and humiliation within a role play for the purpose of generating sexual pleasure. Dominants (sadists) inflict pain while submissives (masochists) receive it.
Safe, sane, and consensual: A phrase used in the S/M community to emphasize and advocate a positive "code of conduct" in the practice of BDSM.
Safe word: An agreed upon word or phrase between participants in any BDSM activity that immediately stops play.
Scene: A play session involving BDSM.
Switch: A person who likes to be both a top and bottom.
Top: Person who is dominant within a scene.
Vanilla: Code word for "not kinky." —SAL

bondage equipment and accessories, for the piercing jewelry, and for so much more. Movie and TV producers come as well. The Noose has been known to furnish costumes for police dramas and porn shoots. It's likely that the dominatrix's outfit you were admiring the other night on cable came from the Noose.

The walls are covered—from floor to ceiling—with whips, chains, harnesses, and other instruments of pain and pleasure. And if you like the smell of leather, you'll love the Noose. The pungent odor smacks you in the face as soon as you set foot in the shop. But don't let the generously endowed stuffed animals, bandanas, and gimmicky lighters throw you. Nothing in this store is for child's play.

While owner Merrill Seldes and her four employees do business with a sizable number of regulars who are deeply immersed in the fetish lifestyle, they relish the opportunity to introduce novices into their world. The knowledgeable and experienced staff is happy to guide any customer through the store and help her make the best purchase. So go ahead, ask away. Nothing you say will surprise the staff.

If the Noose doesn't have what you're looking for, just ask. Many items can be special ordered. Since some of the merchandise is imported from Italy, England, Holland, and Germany, be prepared to wait for a few weeks. And if midnight fetish fever overcomes you, don't fret. The Noose operates a small store within the Lure (409 W. 13th Street), an S/M bar in the West Village. That shop is open from 10:30pm until 3am.   —GM

Paddles

260 West 26th Street between 7th and 8th Avenues
212-629-1854
Fridays: 10pm–4am, Saturdays: 10pm–5am

A LONG TUNNEL—PURPLE-LIT WALLS COVERED with cryptic graffiti—leads down an intimidating flight of

> You don't appreciate a lot
> of stuff in school until you
> get older. Little things
> like being spanked every day
> by a middle-aged woman:
> stuff you pay good money for
> in later life.
>
> —Emo Philips,
> comedian

stairs into Paddles, the world's friendliest S/M club. Paddles is the kind of place that restores your faith in humanity—it's comforting, diverse, and the patrons aren't the least bit judgmental. Amiable Paddles regulars are only too happy to take you on a tour of the cavernous club. There are two floors, numerous rooms (some semi-private), and enough types of apparatus to satisfy anyone's deviant desires. The well-maintained equipment is covered in top-quality black leather. Playthings include a suspended cage, bondage tables, spanking horses, and tons of wall/ceiling restraints.

Much of Paddles's success is owed to its conscientious owner, Michael—master spanker and top—who goes out of his way to keep his patrons happy. For example, he has introduced designated non-smoking areas for customers who like their asses red, but want to keep their lungs pink. Master Michael runs a clean establishment, quite devoid of the sleaze factor that often makes other S/M clubs so unpleasant. Unwanted advances and public masturbation are discouraged, and a word from the owner is usually enough to squash problems before they escalate.

You can dress as elaborately or skimpily as you wish, and a coat check is available should you want to shed your duds entirely. You'll see all types here, from newbies bundled up in winter sweaters to scantily clad dommes decked out in sexy vinyl to nearly naked subs in black leather g-strings. There is a refreshing mix of people—different

Slave for a Day

'M SITTING ON A METAL FOLDING CHAIR WAITING FOR my dominatrix in one of Steel Pavilion's two "holding pens"—tiny, closet-sized rooms adorned with little more than some fetish magazines and a dim light bulb. Through the wall of the neighboring pen, I hear the muddled voices of another client and Mistress Mia—the owner of Steel Pavilion. Next I detect the sound of footsteps. A moment later, Mistress Jackie Guns, a tattooed Bettie Page lookalike, slowly opens the door to my pen.

Dressed in a tight leather shirt adorned with NYPD patches and sporting thigh-high, platform, stiletto boots, Mistress Jackie towers above me. Though we discussed my interests (bondage, discipline, role play) on the phone a few days ago, Jackie wants to review our conversation and prime me on some BDSM basics like safe words ("yellow" means slow down; "red" means stop), just in case I feel overwhelmed. We settle on enacting the following role play: I'm a pot smoking high school truant and Jackie is the cop who's busting me.

Unlike most of New York City's dungeons, Steel Pavilion is not a commercial house—that is, it does not employ a staff of "tops" that work assigned days and shifts. Instead, mistresses and masters with their own clientele rent space at this midtown dungeon, which Mistress Mia spent three months designing and renovating. The play spaces are impressive. One features wall-to-wall thick blue mats, and is dedicated to wrestling. Two large studios with beautiful gold and green speckled walls; dark, hardwood floors; oriental rugs, and tidy closets full of whips, floggers, and other tools are separated by floating doors that can be opened to create a larger space. One contains what looks like a large, black massage table, as well as a chic red velvet and stainless steel throne that doubles as a toilet for submissives into scat play or water sports. The second studio, in which my session was to take place, featured a rusty yet sturdy iron maiden. Yet another room, used for TV (transvestite) scenes, houses a closet full of frilly lingerie and dresses, an antique vanity table, an ironing board for house-servant play, and a medical examination table for different kinds of penetration punishment.

With a flashlight, Mistress Jackie leads me down a deep purple hallway dotted with gargoyle-shaped sconces to a dimly lit studio. Danzig is blaring from the stereo. I expect her to start barking orders, drill-sergeant style, but instead she calmly commands me to strip and kneel, with my head bowed and arms behind my back. I follow her directions.

Mistress Jackie asks me why I'm not in class, and trying to best play the role of a class-cutting stoner, I stutter one lame excuse after another, like, "I was, um, getting groceries for my grandmother." The cop whispers, "I think you're lying," but she can tell I'm a good girl who doesn't normally disobey school rules, so my punishment won't be that severe. She gently bends me over her lap and spanks me once on each cheek, then hits me again and again, each time harder than the last, until my eyes well up with tears. She doesn't, however, feel that I've fully repented for my misbehavior, so my castigation continues.

Mistress Jackie straps and ropes me into a leather harness, hooking me up to a pulley system hanging from the ceiling. As she pulls on the ropes, I slowly ascend until I'm hovering a few feet above the ground. With her (fake) handgun, the mistress torments me by stimulating my clitoris until I'm wet and quivering; then she removes her police baton from her weapon belt and penetrates me with it. I'm sighing and moaning, though, try as I might, it's difficult for me to slide myself up and down on the baton. Mistress Jackie brings me down from the suspension system and orders me to lie down on a doctor's table and handcuffs me. As she resumes screwing me with the nightstick, Beethoven's Ninth Symphony, the "Ode to Joy," swells in the background.

After I've left a good-sized puddle of my juices on the examination table, the mistress removes my handcuffs and massages away any discomfort from my wrists. She gives me a hug and I'm free to go. —EH

races, different bodies, young, old, gorgeous, and average looking—and the male-female ratio is just about 50-50. While the crowd appears to be primarily straight, we saw plenty of bi, lesbian, and transexual frolickers. A night for boy-loving boys is in the works. By the way, gawkers need not attend.

Regular patrons are fiercely loyal and communal, but definitely not cliquey. First-timers shouldn't be afraid to chat them up. They tend to be quite gregarious and will not only tell you whether they're a top, bottom, or switch, but will likely tell you about their favorite TV show, where they went to college, and how they keep razor rash at bay.

Oh, and after you wear out your flogging arm on that sexy, panting masochist, stop by the Whips & Licks Café for a two-dollar coke, cookies, and nachos. Paddles doesn't serve alcohol so if you must drink, take your swigs before showing up.

FYI, every Friday, the first 50 women receive free paddles and on the first Saturday of the month, the club hosts an over the knee spanking party, which gets underway at 8pm; ladies wearing a schoolgirl uniform get in free. Check the club's website for a schedule of upcoming special events.   —*CV*

Pandora's Box
250 West 26th Street between 7th and 8th Avenues
212-242-4577
24 hours a day 7 days a week
Membership: $35; sessions: $185/hour
www.punishmentsquare.com/pandorasbox/enter.html
mrpbox@hotmail.com

AFTER SIX YEARS IN THE FLATIRON DISTRICT, Pandora's Box recently moved to this larger Chelsea location. The new space has no windows, which seems fitting for a dungeon, and the entrance is marked with nothing more than the scripted initials PB. In the reception area—

which is dimly lit and soothingly quiet—we meet Zoë, the manager on duty, who graciously explains the procedures and shows us the rooms in the new space.

Down a narrow, amber-lit hallway are two consultation rooms, both of which are furnished with large, plush chairs, and a few of the mistresses' portfolios lying out for inspection. As we browse through the books, we come across experts in domination, forced feminization, medical play, and a variety of fetishes. Clients can choose from among 30 extremely beautiful mistresses. Next on the tour are the actual Pandora's "boxes"—the fantasy rooms.

The Ming Palace throne room is romantically moody, with a large gold dais at one end, an electronic suspension rig in the center, and low, cushioned platforms on either side. The many antiques play nicely against the red and gold walls. Pass through the leather, wood, and copper-studded double doors and you'll find yourself in the Chinese torture room, which has a custom built red and leather rack, a lacquered restraining chair, a large wheel, and a cell for "puppy" training.

In the Sanctum—a space inspired by Gothic churches—one fully expects to come face to face with members of the Spanish Inquisition. The walls are roughhewn stone lit solely by flames emanating from iron wall fixtures. Medieval torture devices, including the Katherine Wheel and the adjustable St. Andrew's cross, sit vacant in anticipation of their next victim. In the adjacent interrogation room, hidden microphones and cameras are poised to capture the humiliating confessions of unsuspecting submissives.

The schoolroom is stark but effective, consisting of a wooden student's desk, a large teacher's desk, and a chalkboard. Paddles, rather than pea jackets, hang from the coat hooks. Next door, of course, is the principal's office—furnished in leather and dark wood paneling—where one can expect more extreme punishment.

The cross-dressing room, also known as the China Doll room, will certainly appeal to men seeking the pleasures—and pains—of corsets, heels, and lingerie. Clients can select their garb from a huge walk-in closet, and then perch at the dressing table to choose a wig and apply their makeup. Or they can lounge on the low couches—surrounded by pink murals of geishas—while trying on stilettos and pumps.

The Medical room, with its hammered-steel, tiled walls and metallic gray gynecologist's table, offers the client a chance to explore a range of healthy pleasures, such as being restrained on a padded gurney or turn of the century wheelchair. A glass and chrome cabinet holds a nightmarish selection of medical tools. Here, you'll also find TENS units (these devices use electrical current to stimulate nerves), single-use medical supplies, and a private, spa bathroom.

Open 24/7, Pandora's Box, offers enough torturous treasures to last a lifetime. *—MU*

Throb

718-574-6751 (call for party location)
Open 8pm-1am—no admission after midnight
Admission: 8pm-9pm $15; 9pm-midnight $20
Held first Thursday of every month; women and "transgendered people in solidarity with the women's community" welcome
http://members.aol.com/throbparty
Subscribe to email list at:
throbparty-subscribe@yahoogroups.com

♀

THROB IS NOT FOR THE FAINT OF HEART. IT'S A power-packed, women's play party where bevies of luscious babes come to act out their kinkiest fantasies. The monthly event regularly attracts over 80 women. Promoters Red Robinson and Tristan Taormino describe Throb attendees as "leatherwomen, S/M-curious women, vanilla chicks, dirty girls, and our trans friends." So you certainly don't have to be 100 percent dyke to attend.

Clearly, women of all sexual orientations come to Throb, where the vibe is relaxed and friendly, and voyeurism is definitely encouraged.

Delicious snacks, along with nonstop porn, are served in the front room where those who've just completed a scene—or anybody for that matter—gather to chat, smoke, or just sit and relax. The scene rooms offer a bit more excitement. Throb offers slings, a St. Andrews cross, a wet room (for those who favor water sports), a back room (where partygoers are encouraged to check their clothes), and assorted toys and equipment. Lube and gloves abound, as safe sex is mandatory. In fact, guests must sign a consent form upon entering, agreeing to certain basic safety rules.

Invariably, crowds gather around the hottest scenes to get a glimpse of flogging, fisting, caning, rope bondage, and other kinky demonstrations. Actually, demos are plentiful, so if you're looking to find out just what that single-tail whip or pretty flogger feels like against your ass, this is the place to go. On one of my visits, a birthday girl lay down on a platform as small candles were placed all over her body. The candles were then lit, and as hot wax dripped onto her flesh, much to her delight, revelers erupted into a chorus of "Happy Birthday."

There are so many women at Throb that if you're looking to play, you can usually find a willing partner (top or bottom). And if you're looking to just…look…you can do that as well. Not an exhibitionist? There are plenty of nooks and crannies, so you can certainly get it on without attracting an audience.

The evening starts to heat up around 10pm. Our suggestion: come early and come often.   —*RKB*

SEX CLUBS & EROTIC-PARTIES

THE DAYS OF PLATO'S RETREAT ARE LONG GONE, AND there are far fewer gay bathhouses now than years ago, but "swinging" (i.e. that somewhat passé term for swapping partners, not dancing to big bands) and going to clubs to have sex, anonymously or with a partner, are still popular pursuits in the Big Apple.

Sex clubs are of two types: on-premises and off-premises. At the latter, the club is merely nominal—couples or multiples actually gather in a home or motel to do the deed. At on-premises clubs, the action takes place at the club, often in full view of all the guests, making these venues a fantasy-come-true for voyeurs and exhibitionists alike.

If you decide to visit a sex club never assume that everyone there is ready to jump your bones at the drop of a g-string. Visitors to these clubs can be as discriminating as people who frequent singles bars. In fact, it's likely that some of the folks you'll meet are merely voyeurs or exhibitionists and have no intention of getting into the sack with anyone—except perhaps their steady partner. And those who do like to swing or have casual sex may want to get to know you socially first, before taking the relationship to a horizontal level.

Behave at a sex club just as you would at a friend's cocktail party. Be polite; don't stare; make small talk, avoid controversial topics like religion and politics; and, most importantly, touch only if invited to do so. If a stranger comes on to you too strongly, just politely tell them that they are making you uncomfortable—usually that's enough to put a halt to their advances. —*TH*

Acquiesce

210 East 23rd Street, 4th floor, between 2nd
and 3rd Avenues
212-696-1007
M, W-Sa: 5:30pm-11:30pm
Single men: $140; couples: $60; single women: $25 ♀♂

ACQUIESCE HAS BEEN IN BUSINESS SINCE THE
early '80s and unlike its competitors, admits single men.
This can be good or bad, depending on what you're kink
is, but for single men it's very, very good. It's especially
good for the club because single guys are its main revenue
source, and to keep them coming back, Acquiesce employs
women (not raving beauties, by the way) to "work" the
crowd each night. As a result, in the words of the owner,
these guys are "guaranteed to get laid."

Located in a former karate studio, Acquiesce does not
dress to impress. What passes for décor are windows covered with black sheets. There are three main rooms: a
lounge area, where porn videos are shown (during our visit,
we were lucky enough to catch a reenactment of John and
Lorraine Bobbit's pivotal moment); a semi-private room
(no door, but it's tucked away off the hall) with a mattress
and what appeared to be (and sounded like) caged para-
keets stored in the rafters; and a large open space with a
half-dozen mattresses strewn about. And, should your
blood sugar take a dip in the course of the evening, there's
a complimentary snack bar with cookies and soda.

We wandered in at around 9:30 pm on a Saturday and
unfortunately had just missed a big party. After changing
out of our street clothes in the unisex dressing room
(where, should your coif need spiffing up, there's a curling
iron at your disposal), we donned towels and went exploring. Alas, despite the early hour, the evening was actually
winding down and there wasn't a great deal to see. All we
encountered were four single men hanging around watching porn videos, and one couple getting it on.

The club is busiest on Mondays and Fridays at 6:30pm.

We'd recommend it for couples who like to show off, single men who aren't getting any, and single women who can't get enough. —*SAL*

The Bijou

82 East 4th Street between 1st and 2nd Avenues
Phone: unlisted
Hours: vary
Admission: $10

♂♂

THE BIJOU, ALSO KNOWN AS CLUB 82, IS NOT LIST-ed in local gay guides, and that is intentional. The management disguises the club (and its sister club, the Jewel) as a family entertainment center showing old movies. This is in response to zoning laws—instituted during the Giuliani administration—that make it illegal for adult entertainment venues to operate in residential neighborhoods. But despite its low profile and genteel façade, the Bijou is in fact in full swing as a sex club, albeit one of the least palatable places for gay men to have public sex in New York.

When it opened in 1989, the Bijou was quite a happening scene, combining within its black-painted, dimly lit basement walls a porn theater, private stalls, and several open areas, all of which were rife with sexual activity when we visited. A coffee urn and soda fountain sat atop a bar dispensing complimentary beverages alongside Oreo cookies and lubricated condoms. A raised platform with a comfy old couch and some bistro tables provided a quiet area away from the frenzy where you could chat with a buddy or just sit and watch from a safe distance. Coin-operated lockers provided for safe deposit of your valuables and outerwear while you enjoyed the club, with no time limit on your stay. By 2am or so, the place would be virtually wall-to-wall with guys getting it on one-on-one or in groups.

Much of that description still applies today, except that the porn videos have been replaced by cheesy old crime dramas and sexual activity is not permitted in the open areas. As before, men populate the private stalls and the corridors outside them, creating a rather grim parade of desperate-looking patrons hoping to get off. The one demonstrable improvement to the establishment is that the bathrooms have been totally renovated, with bright lighting, clean tile, and doors that close. But while clean bathrooms are nice as a general rule, there was something to be said for the grungy old toilets in cramped wooden stalls that characterized the old Bijou—you somehow felt that the sexual adventure continued, even during pit stops.

The Bijou is largely about sucking dick, or getting your dick sucked. Men in the private stalls generally indicate their proclivities by the position they assume—bottoms generally sit on the hard wooden bench, while tops lean against the wall or in the doorway, one thumb hooked in their jeans pocket, the other hand groping their crotch. Once the door to the private stall is closed, however, anything can happen.

If the Bijou has any charm, it is in its seedy, glory-hole ambiance. There are certainly cleaner, brighter, better equipped places to have sex with strangers in New York.

But if you like the idea of walking into that private stall, closing the door behind you, and unbuckling your belt without a word as you advance on the man seated on the bench in front of you (or sitting on that bench yourself)—go ahead, knock yourself out. —*MHB*

CAKE
212-591-1994
www.cakenyc.com
cake@cakenyc.com

ON A THURSDAY EVENING IN EARLY NOVEMBER, a group of women are lined up outside a neighborhood bar. They're not overly manicured nor are they especially young. They're professionals—confident and hip without pretension and most noticeably sexy. So where are the men?

Inside the bar, is where. Dressed in various costumes and sharing a bottle of scotch, a small group of guys are engaged in banter as a chrome pole is erected in the middle of a stage. The motley crew—dressed as firemen, suits, pretty boys, and rockers—seem a bit ragged as one by one they enthusiastically but clumsily attempt to slide down the pole.

Then the doors open. The women rush in. This is the first female-only event in CAKE's history: CAKE Lapdance—an all-amateur male lap dancing party in which the men give lap dances to the women.

The MC, Emily Scarlet Kramer, a co-founder of CAKE, welcomes the crowd and states the rules for lap dances: dancers must do exactly what the women request; the minimum per dance is set at ten dollars, a bargain by normal strip venue standards. Then Emily

Manhunt Party

URING NEW YORK'S GAY PRIDE WEEKEND, THOUSANDS of tourists invade the city to celebrate their right to party and most of the men kick it all off on Friday at the annual Manhunt Party. This testosterone packed, no-holds-barred event began in 1994 and has become the traditional starting point for studs on the prowl and seems to get a little bit wilder every year.

Manhunt is a great way to get a fresh look at the fresh meat before three days of indulgence leaves the merchandise a little torn and frayed. The quality of the crowd, say the producers, is the main focus of the party. "We concentrate very heavily on marketing the event to men who are friendly, but who also happen to be the cream of the crop. Yeah, it's shallow, but this isn't exactly the party where the guests discuss politics or the economy."

The first few Manhunts drew heavily on the artistic talents of Tom of Finland and Colt Studios; now the event is updating its look by incorporating the work of other erotic artists. However, it's doubtful you'll give much consideration to the party's aesthetics, especially with distractions like a live x-rated photo

introduces the dancers: Nick No, Aries, Achilles, and the rest who comically greet their audience—no macho posturing here. They perform on stage, one by one, before heading into the audience to try their hand at lap dances.

The first dancer, Nick No, is a cute '70s mop-top with a satin pink baseball jacket, a tweed golf cap, and the best butt of the night. He gyrates and mounts the pole—wildly imitating Mick Jagger—and strips off several pairs of skivvies. The women yell and cheer him on. When his dance is done, he is quickly besieged for several lap dances.

Elated (if a bit terrified), the dancers revel in the attention being showered upon them. No matter that most of them move like Tom Cruise in *Risky Business*. The cheese factor is not only tolerated, but welcomed by these women

shoot with porn stars (you can probably even fool around with the performers after they've finished working) and a 12-foot papier-mâché cock that you can dance under.

The event is famous for the frisky, naughty nature of its crowd, and the popular Manhunt scavenger hunt—which features super sexy clues—will likely make the revelers that much friskier. Contestants will vie for a variety prizes including a night with a famous escort. You can also enter a contest to be a "Manhunt host." When pressed for details as to the official host duties, the producers said, "Please. It's a beauty contest. You stand around, look pretty, drink for free, and have hot men throw themselves at you. What else do you want?"

For party specifics and contest details go to www.manhuntparty.com. —*TR*

212 529-4130
June 28, 2002
Location to be announced
$50 advance/$60 at door
www.manhuntparty.com
info@manhuntparty.com

who appreciate the dancers' sweet enthusiasm and their eagerness to please. The audience shows its gratitude with cheers. Some women spray whip cream and beer on the performers' bodies. Others lap it up.

Next up is the Big Balls contest—men arm wrestling in their underwear. Women place wagers and the winners receive a private dance on stage. Somewhere in the back of the bar, a VIP area is set up for women who want to indulge in very long, very sensual lap dances. The climax of the evening is *The Full Monty* bidding. When the results are in, a few dancers bare it all to the delight of the crowd.

Finally, at 2am, the event is proclaimed officially over. The stage is now a sorry sight—melting whip cream commingles with puddles of beer and discarded clothing.

CAKE, the host of the event, is a New York-based entertainment and production company that caters to heterosexual women. The company's founders, Melinda Gallagher (president) and Emily Scarlet Kramer (web development director), have formal education in women's health and sexuality, and experience advocating for women's issues. Their monthly events—which are uncensored and permit men to attend only if escorted by a woman—aim to help women become more comfortable with their sexuality. Annual favorites include the Striptease-a-Thon, during which a woman can try their hand at taking it off, and the Cake Forum, which features readings by writers of erotica as well as writing workshops for attendees.

At CAKE's website, www.cakenyc.com, women can apply for a CAKE Card and sign up for the CAKE newsletter. They can also respond to the latest CAKE survey, submit an erotic story to Surrender the Pink, check out the editorials, or take a look at pics from previous events. CAKE is also an excellent resource for information on various issues of relevance to women.

CAKE's tagline reads: "Sexy. Moist. Sticky. Hot. Juicy. Sweet. Tasty. Yummy", and indeed, there is something at CAKE for every woman's taste.   —*MU*

Carousel Club

South Street Seaport area

212-252-2138; 917-755-6930

♀♂ ♀

For location, hours, or directions, call from 8pm-10pm
weekdays or 8pm-5am Saturdays

Saturdays: 10pm-5am

$80 per couple; $40, single women; quarterly membership:
$20; only couples and single women are admitted

www.geocities.com/clubcarousel/welcome.html

AFTER RECEIVING A TIP FROM SOME VETERAN
swingers that Carousel was worth a visit, we made the trip to
Manhattan's Financial District one snowy Saturday eve
arriving just after midnight eager to view the action. By that
time of night, we figured, the party would be in full, er,
swing, but alas, the manager explained that the harsh weather discouraged many patrons. On a typical Saturday, he said,
40 to 60 couples would be in attendance, but he estimated
that only about half that many would show up that night.
He was right. And his prediction was a clear tip-off that
most of the couples that visit Carousel are from the outer
boroughs and beyond (the other tip-off is the extensive list
of driving directions included in the club's standard e-mail
correspondence).

No matter that the crowd was small—we were out to
have a good time. After registering at the front desk, we
each grabbed a comfy terry robe, took a tour of the cavernous club, and then retired to our respective lockers
(patrons are given a key to a locker where valuables can be
stored) to get ready for a night of fun and frolic. You can
keep your clothes on all night if you prefer, but no sneak-
ers, jeans, or shorts are allowed.

Carousel is huge. The place sprawls over three levels
and clearly has the potential to host an awesome baccha-
nal. Some have even compared it to Plato's Retreat, which,
in its heyday—the late '70s—was a swinger's paradise. The
problem, however, is that on a slow night Carousel is way
too big. Without a large crowd to mingle with, you feel as

though you've wandered into a bizarre game of erotic hide and seek. We were informed however, that just a few weeks after our visit, no less than 86 couples were in attendance and every playroom was packed with writhing bodies!

On the club's first level, which overlooks the main lounging area, a competent DJ spins an assortment of dance tracks throughout the evening. If there's a particular song that really gets your motor running, you'll be happy to know that he takes requests.

The facilities include a pool room (as in billiards); a dimly lit play area lined with chairs (musical chairs anybody?); another play area with mats and exercise equipment (just in case you get the urge to do a workout); an Olympic-size swimming pool (nude volleyball anyone?) with an adjacent hot tub; a pub-like lounge area with a hot tub and a glass-paneled sauna big enough for three to four couples; and finally, an enormous main mingling room which features a hot and cold buffet and soft drinks (you can BYOB but be advised that alcohol—and drugs—are a very bad idea at a sex party), plus a giant-screen TV, which unfortunately was tuned to the Robin Byrd show (we were hoping for porn videos). Man, just describing this place is exhausting and we certainly got plenty of exercise wandering to and from one play area to the next.

The sparse crowd consisted mostly of thirty- and forty-somethings from the suburbs. Nearly all had donned robes or towels while a few stayed clothed. We found some of the couples attractive, but none of them really blew us away (figuratively that is), and the guests were not especially chatty. Perhaps, having traveled to the Carousel in a snowstorm, they were still thawing out.

What we liked most about the club was that it offered us the opportunity to have sex in so many different, cool settings. The sauna was hot in more ways than one, and it was especially fun to be spied on by the couples on the opposite side of the glass enclosure and vice versa. The billiards room was also a major turn-on and gave an entirely new meaning to the term pool hustler. But our favorite play area turned out to be a massage room (complete with professional massage table), which was adjacent to the ladies locker room.

By 3:30am we decided to call it quits, and although we didn't indulge with any other couples during the course of the evening, we certainly felt as though we had gotten our money's worth. In short, whether you're a tried and true swinger, a voyeur, or an exhibitionist, Carousel has the potential to fulfill your sexual fantasies. But before you go, check the weather forecast, and if snow is in the cards, rent a movie instead. —*TH*

Checkmates

227 East 56th Street between 2nd and 3rd Avenues
212-421-3313
F-Sa: 9pm-4am
Admission: $100 per couple; membership
fee: $20 (valid for three months)

♀♂

AN ON-PREMISES SWING CLUB IN A NON-DESCRIPT commercial building smack in the middle of midtown? Yes, just a few short blocks from ultra-posh Sutton Place, Checkmates offers merry swapsters a comfortable space for fun and frolic. At the same address, you'll also find the East Side Club, a gay bathhouse (see entry below). We accidentally took the elevator there at first, but quickly discovered our mistake.

Upon arriving at Checkmates you may feel that you're about to board an international flight. The bouncer will check your ID (you must be over 21), have you fill out some paperwork (for liability concerns perhaps), and pay. Each couple receives a locker equipped with a robe. If you choose to disrobe you must do so in tandem. You must also get dressed at the same time. The locker attendant was an extremely jovial and efficient Irish ex-pat. Any time we needed to retrieve something, such as a condom, we would wander over to our locker, and voila, there he'd be.

The club has a sort of late '70s/early '80s feel. The spartan décor is glitzy, and a bit cheesy—but in a fun way.

Performance Anxiety

CONCERNED ABOUT YOUR PERFORMANCE IN BED? Feel like you're craving sex all the time or hardly at all? Never seem to reach the big "O", or get there in ten seconds flat? Consider getting some professional help. While psychotherapists can offer assistance in contending with such issues, you will likely be best served seeking advice from someone who is specially trained to help clients with sexual dysfunction. Through the American Association of Sex Educators, Counselors and Therapists' website—www.aasect.org—you can locate a certified counselor or therapist in the New York City area. The site also offers numerous links to other helpful organizations. —EC

Balloons are strewn all over the central gathering area as though it were New Year's Eve. There's a "stripper's pole" in the middle of the small dance area and off to the sides are a small buffet (we didn't partake as we had just had dinner) and a bar (we did partake, but a word to the wise: always stay sober at a sex party). XXX videos play non-stop on two monitors. Toward the rear of the club are four "party" rooms. These are essentially bedrooms with futon mattresses on wooden frames and some modular foam furniture. There are also showers and two very clean restrooms. In fact the whole place was virtually spotless.

Feeling a bit self-conscious at first, we both grabbed a glass of wine and chatted up the friendly and very attractive bartender, who, it turned out, was an actress. No surprise there. By 10pm, the crowd was still rather sparse, but definitely diverse. Most of the couples were attractive and appeared to be in their 30s and 40s, some perhaps a bit younger. They were approachable, but not overly friendly and you got the sense that most of them were cautiously checking each other out like prizefighters in the early rounds of a match.

Couples continued to arrive and one by one retire to the back rooms. At one point, three drop-dead gorgeous women showed up with a tall, studly-looking guy. They wasted no time taking over the dance floor and shedding their clothes. We were later informed by the locker attendant that all three of the women had posed for a major men's magazine. We wouldn't doubt it. One of the women asked us if we had been to a swing club before. We had in fact and said as much, but in retrospect wished we had said, "No. Would you show us how it's done?"

We had another glass of wine and then made the rounds of the bedrooms. At first, we just observed the scene. It was tough to tell if anybody was actually "swinging" but there's no doubt they were having sex. In one room, an eye-catching threesome was happily going at it. The lone male was penetrating a woman from behind while she lapped between her partner's thighs. Since we weren't exactly in a swapping mood, we decided to commandeer the middle bedroom for ourselves. Every so often couples would come in to watch us. And at one point an older couple approached, asking if we'd like to join them, but we politely declined. Fortunately, nobody saw us topple the bed over. Be careful, those wooden frames aren't too stable!

Towards the end of the evening, the club and yours truly petered out. We chatted up the bartender again, had a final glass of wine, and then went on our merry way. All in all, Checkmates gets two thumbs—or whatever—up.   —*TH*

East Side Club

227 East 56th Street between 2nd and 3rd Avenues
212-753-2222
24 hours a day, 7 days a week
Annual membership card (required for admission): $30; day pass: $10; room rental (4 hours): $16; changing room (4 hours): $14; locker charge: $11; (note that prices are $2 higher from 2pm Friday until Sunday at midnight)

THE EAST SIDE CLUB BILLS ITSELF, RATHER VAGUELY, as a "private men's club." The fact is it's a bathhouse—

a place for men to have sex with other men—catering to a mature clientele with lots of gray hair and not a lot of muscle. Most "out" gay men do not frequent such establishments because they have no reason to keep their affairs secret. They'd rather stride into a bar or coffee house, meet a guy, strike up a conversation, and perhaps take him home. Ah, home. There's the rub. We noticed a number of men sporting wedding rings at the East Side Club. Enough said.

The club is an attractive place with subdued lighting, marbled floors and a soothing color scheme of deep blues. There are three floors that are subdivided into "rooms," changing rooms, and locker areas. The walls of the rooms and changing rooms don't quite reach the ceiling, although they are fitted with regular, lockable doors. The rooms, typically, are really no bigger than a walk-in closet, and are furnished with a sheeted bed. The changing rooms are pretty much the same, only with a bench instead of a bed. The locker room resembles that of virtually any high school in America, minus the kids of course.

Patrons rent a room or locker, disrobe, don a towel, and start cruising. There are several open seating areas, as well as an area with video monitors featuring round-the-clock porno. Some patrons just cruise up and down the hallways, peering into those rooms whose doors are open. Body language is the language of choice at clubs like

> Sex without love is an empty experience, but as empty excperiences go, it's one of the best.
>
> —Woody Allen

this—virtually no words are exchanged. Men make eye contact and suggestive motions if they're interested in each other. If there's a match, well...

The East Side Club also has a small steam room and sauna, as well as decent toilet and shower facilities. A word of etiquette, however: there is no cruising in the toilet areas. Given that every other area in this club is designed for sex, it seems only fair to leave alone those guys who really just want to answer nature's call. After all, they do need some privacy. —*MJN*

J's Hangout

675 Hudson Street at 14th Street
212-242-9292
Daily: midnight-8am
Admission: M-Th: $10; F-Sa (and holidays): $15; $5 discount on Saturdays with any gym membership ID

Special Parties:
New York Jacks (jerk-off party for men; nudity is required)
Mondays: 8pm-midnight, doors close at 10pm
Thursdays: 5pm-9pm, doors close at 7pm
$10; $8 for members of New York Jacks (www.nyjacks.com)

New York Bondage Club (www.nybondageclub.com)
Fridays: 8pm-midnight (doors close at 9pm); $15

Foot Friends foot fetish party (www.footfriends.com)
2nd Saturday of the month; 8pm-12midnight;
doors close at 10pm; $15

THE STEEL DOOR IS OPEN ONLY DURING THE SPECI-fied hours. The entrance is easy to miss, especially if you're not looking for it. Just inside the door, there's a cashier to whom you pay a cover charge, after which the inner door is opened. It's sort of like a speakeasy, only much different.

On a regular night, the atmosphere at J's can be intimidating to anyone without an edge and a tough attitude. The interior is painted black. There's plenty of built-in

two-tiered wooden bench seating along the wall in the bar area. Further back is a pool table, with an adjacent sofa-seating area. Glance at the video monitors above and you'll be treated to non-stop male porn flicks.

In the center of everything is a dance floor with a DJ and disco ball. Hardly anyone dances, however, as this dance floor is for cruising. The stairway at the back of the dance floor leads to two dimly-lit, cave-like rooms that appear to be hewn out of stone. Inside, all inhibitions are lifted and, wordlessly, men indulge in each other in every conceivable position. A bouncer keeps guard to ensure the rooms don't get overfilled (the smaller of the rooms, about 9 feet square, has been seen to hold as many as 20 men at one time).

Back upstairs, there's refreshment in the form of water and soft drinks. J's Hangout does not have a liquor license. Beverages are $2, $1 before 2am, and free to any man who wears nothing but a jock strap or briefs (clothing check is free). In case you were wondering, the restroom facilities are decent. —MJN

Le Trapeze

17 East 27th Street between Madison and 5th Avenues
212-532-0298
W-Sa: 9pm-close
Admission: $115/couple: F-Sa; $105/couple: W-Th (includes
3-month membership card; subsequent visits within
3 months are $85 on F-Sa and $75 on W-Th)
Only heterosexual couples are admitted

FOR MOST OF THE 20TH CENTURY, THE MADISON Pub was a beloved neighborhood watering hole housed within the landmark Prince George Hotel (built in 1903). In 1980, the pub's quarters were taken over by the swing club, Le Trapeze (the old-time regulars must be turning in their graves). To their credit, the owners of Le Trapeze have retained much of the Madison's original cozy interior. The wood ceilings, brick walls, stained glass windows, and wagon-wheel chandeliers have been spared the demolition ball, while modern touches such as a dance floor, mood lighting, and disco balls have been added.

The vibe at Le Trapeze is that of a local coffeehouse brimming with friendly regulars. In the dining and lounge area near the entrance, couples alternately chat and sip sodas, fill up on the hot and cold buffet (sex machines need fuel), and exchange contact information on memo pads placed near the couches and tables. Above the bar, porn films are playing, and most of the 150 or so customers who come and go throughout the evening are wearing only towels or playful underwear. Guests range in age from 20s to 60s and come in all colors, shapes, and sizes.

After undressing in the locker room and shower area (couples must disrobe and dress together), we scouted the large "group activity room," then stopped by a smaller nook with mirrored walls to watch an attractive foursome grope, lick, and suck each other to quivering ecstasy while nearby, two other couples were engaged in sexual gymnastics. In the mood to jump into the action, we investigated the four private rooms, hoping that we'd find an unlocked door and an opportunity to join a group grope, but alas this was not to be.

Still determined to participate, we made our way up the spiral staircase, slipping past the warm, naked bodies of curious patrons. We peeked into a half-dozen semi-private rooms (think very small motel room that others can get access to) where plenty of multiple partner acrobatics were taking place. The most enticing space upstairs contained two "love seats"—chairs that could have been designed by a sex-crazed physician. They allow guests—usually women—to lie back and be pleasured by whomever they choose.

Turned on and inspired by the barrage of sighs, groans, and moans, we settled into an enjoyable ménage a trois in one of the upstairs rooms. What a fitting conclusion—and climax—for a memorable evening. —*EH*

EROTIC

Mt. Morris Baths

1944 Madison Avenue between 124th and 125th Streets
212-534-9004
Open 24 hours, 7 days a week
Rooms: $19; Walk-ins: $16; Lockers: $10; (rates are for
12 hours on weekdays and 8 hours on weekends)

Mt. Morris Baths (or The Mount as it's fam-
iliarly known) is considered a landmark among black sex
spaces. Even after a bad visit, The Mount's ghoulish charm
draws you back. It survived the panic-induced, shutdown
of bathhouses that swept through New York and the Bay
Area during the start of the AIDS crisis in the '80s.

The Liberty Inn

JUST LISTENING TO THE RECORDED MESSAGE WHEN
you phone the Liberty Inn for directions, rates, and hours
is an erotic experience. The voice on the other end of the
line is soothing and seductive, assured and dominating.
The automated description of the premises is so thorough that
when I toured the place with manager Richard Boyd, I felt that I
already knew what to expect at this petite three-story love motel
on the western fringe of Greenwich Village.

At the front desk, the clerk could not be more disinterested in
your business. He's too involved in the latest John Grisham
novel—which is just as well. He asks how long you want to
stay—by the hour or more—and assigns you a room.

Most of the rooms are cozy—furnishings include a bed, chair,
and table—and very clean. During my visit, the maintenance staff
was frenetically vacuuming and changing sheets; they are
trained to turn out a spotless room in only 10 minutes. TV's hang
from a ceiling corner or sit on a shelf (The Liberty has five in-
house adult channels) and the private bathrooms are equipped
with towels, soap, and hair dryers. The decor is spartan, but tasteful—down to the headboards—which are designed by Boyd's
wife. Most rooms have mirrors on the walls and/or ceiling, which
are great fun for narcissists and voyeurs. And several of the

Somehow, this place managed to stay open, whether because of longevity, the owner's connections, or the fact that it is also used as a shelter by men with nowhere else to go.

At the gate, there's a rickety old sign that reads "Mount Morris Turkish Baths: Men Only." If you are lucky, the line to get in will be short. The place is notorious for long waits caused by an elaborate processing procedure and the need to mop up vacated rooms.

Once processed, you get your key, as well as condoms and lube (you can always go back for more), and a towel. You then proceed to your choice of "accommodations." Unless you are planning a short stay (one or two

rooms actually feature hand-painted ceilings by a well-known Chinese muralist. Air purifiers are standard. You can request a whirlpool or waterbed for an additional $5.

If you get a little low on glycogen or fluids after your first round of frolicking, vending machines in the lobby dispense Oreos, Snickers, Coke, and Poland Spring, as well as condoms and Tylenol. —SES

51 10th Avenue at 14th Street
212-741-2333
$53-$69: 3-hour stay (including tax); call for overnight rates; first come, first serve—reservations not accepted
www.libertyinnnyc.com

hours) and/or are pretty sure that people will invite you to their rooms or walk-ins, your best bet would be to get a room or walk-in of your own. The wait for a room is typically much longer than for a walk-in, so you have to decide if it's worth it. Rooms are a bit larger than the single beds they contain. Walk-ins—not the most comfortable option, but still private—are basically closet-size with a built-in wooden bench. If you opt for a locker only, you can use the dorm-style bunk beds in the public area.

Often characterized as a dump, Mt. Morris has made a few improvements in recent years. More rooms were added to alleviate the long waits, but some folks complain that the only other visible renovation consisted of the addition of linoleum floors.

The clientele is mostly black and Latino with a smattering of Asian and white men. Once in a while a group scene develops in the sauna or steam room and occasionally there are threesomes in the rooms, but there is no space for group action in the walk-ins.

Room occupants leave their doors open to display what they've got—you'll see patrons sticking their asses out or playing with their dicks, or simply sitting and checking out the procession of customers (in towels or boxers) outside their rooms to decide with whom they want to hook up. Others will cruise the sauna, steam room, or TV areas in search of a partner. On a good visit, you don't have to leave your door open for long or walk around much. On a bad night, though, you best be wearing comfortable shoes as you might be doing a whole lot of walking.

Mt. Morris is worth checking out at least once, if only for its historical significance. This reviewer's experience has been more miss than hit, but a good visit, I'm told, can be truly mind-blowing. —*NN*

Michele Capozzi's Erotic Tours

FILMMAKER, JOURNALIST, PRODUCER, "PORNOLO-gist" and urban explorer, Michele (pronounced Mee-kay-lay) Capozzi is the consummate tour guide. Born in Genoa, Michele has his finger firmly planted on New York City's throbbing pulse and is well acquainted with all of Gotham's underground hot spots as well as with the political, economic, and social vagaries of the city. His marathon tours enable participants to see people and places that they may have only fantasized about. Michele will not only escort you to exotic locales, including trans-vestite bars, S/M clubs, and underground after-hours joints, but will also introduce you to the people and personalities that make these places sizzle. He is known and is loved by virtually everybody in this erotic underground. His running commentary is both amusing and informative and makes for a most enjoyable evening.

Michele prefers to keep his tour groups small—a married couple, two men, a mother and daughter, for example. The fewer the people, the more places one can visit and the more intimate the experience. Tours can be personalized according to the tastes of the participants and prices are worked out during the consultation phase, but prepared to shell out at least a few big bills. Day tours are also available and focus primarily on the city's fascinating ethnic enclaves. For more information, or to arrange a tour, call 212-580-2219. Please note that Mr. Capozzi travels exten-sively and occasionally leaves New York for lengthy busi-ness trips. —*TH*

212-580-2219

EROTIC

One Leg Up

Party locations and themes vary;
check website for details
$130 per couple
www.oneleggupnyc.com
yourleg@oneleggupnyc.com

⚥

THE FOUNDER OF ONE LEG UP, THE BEAUTIFUL
Palagia, made it very clear to us that she throws erotic parties, not swing parties. Her goal is to bring together intelligent, attractive, and sexy guests for a night of fun and
frolic; swapping partners is not the objective, although
this is certainly not discouraged. Palagia prides herself on
selecting elegant venues, serving delicious food, and creating a truly erotic ambiance. To ensure the right mix of
guests, she handpicks the partygoers (prospective attendees must pass an elaborate screening process which
includes the submission of a photo and the completion of
an essay on what makes them and their partner hot).

Each party has a specific theme and we were licking
our lips in anticipation of the Blow party, which, yes,
focused on oral pleasure. Tight security is observed. Two
days before the party, we received via e-mail that night's
password—"eat me"—that we would need for admission.
We also were sent a general address, but had to call a special hotline the evening of the event to find out exactly
where the party was being held.

We reached our destination on the Lower East Side a
little after 10:30pm and were the first guests to arrive.
This gave us an opportunity to talk with the hostess, bartender, and staff, all of whom were very friendly, and
scope out each new arrival. After checking our coats, we
explored the space, a large and stunning loft apartment,
illuminated mainly by candlelight. In the bathroom,
oodles of Blow Pops (suckers with gum in the center)
were stuffed into the tumbler by the sink, a cute reminder
of the event's theme.

A small bar, complete with a shirtless male bartender,

was set up in the kitchen, and a gorgeous spread of berries, spinach pies, biscotti, and other delicacies was laid out in a nook off the living room. One by one the mostly youngish couples arrived (more than 20 at the party's peak), and on the whole they were quite an attractive and ethnically diverse lot. Entertaining the crowd were two low-key erotic dancers—one male and one female—presumably hired by the hostess. A well-chosen selection of music also helped to set the mood.

The vibe was comfortable—like a cocktail party at a friend's home—in comparison to some of the commercial swing venues we had visited. Most people were smartly dressed, although to be sure décolletage, exposed breasts, spiked heels, and fishnet stockings were in evidence. We felt comfortable talking with other couples, mostly about how they had heard about the venue and where else they had partied.

A bit after midnight, the hostess started recruiting volunteers for the Blow Contest. The winner would be the man with the loudest orgasm. We were among ten couples participating, and while apparently there was a winner within minutes, we couldn't gauge the decibel level of his orgasm, nor did we really care. We were having too much fun to notice.

After the contest, the level of play intensified somewhat, but there wasn't a great deal of visible sex. One of the attendees noted "there's less sex tonight than at the last party, but more intimacy." One couple that had eyed us earlier in the evening finally found two willing partners, but after a few minutes it was obvious they were just going through the motions.

We were approached a few times by couples, but never made it beyond some light stroking, except when the female member of our group was trapped in a secluded nook by a horny couple and the coat check fellow. We refrained from playing more because of the absence of comfortable horizontal space (although we later learned that most of One Leg Up's parties are held in large lofts with gobs of lounging space). Standing or sitting is okay

Russian & Turkish Baths

THROUGH THE DREAMY, SOFTLY LIT HAZE OF THE steam room, strangers lounge and moan softly in the ferocious, dark heat of the Russian shvitz. Alright, so even if most of them are fat, old Russian guys, the experience of these baths remains a sensual and quintessential New York experience.

Despite the occasional downtown hipster, toy boy, or appealing couple, this bathhouse remains relatively true to its Eastern European origins. While wheat grass juice and smoothies are now available alongside pork dumplings, borscht, and blintzes, this place remains more Old World than New Age. Frankly the baths haven't aged all that gracefully in their 110 years. The locker rooms are musty and cramped; the showers reek of industrial disinfectant; the dun-colored robes are shapeless and unflattering; and icky plastic slippers are mandatory. Still, the place has genuine character and sure can chase the blues away on a cold winter afternoon. An outdoor sun deck and cheap beer entice in the summer.

Four types of baths are the enticements: an electric or "Turkish" hammam; a steam room (wet heat); a redwood, Finnish sauna; and the epic Russian bath or shvitz—followed by a dip in an ice-cold pool. There's something almost medieval about the bath's most popular and best-known Russian room where you'll find a massive stone chimney blasting at a fierce 195 degrees, men and women in monkish robes and towel turbans sighing faintly in the dim light, and—in one corner—prone victims being beaten by two burly men with bunches of oak leaves attached to stout sticks, as if taking part in some kind of public martyrdom ritual. This type of "massage", platza, is meant to bring toxins to the surface of the skin, to be immediately sweated out in the dry heat, and the oak leaves and olive oil soap they're soaked in are said to have natural astringent properties. Similarly brutal massages—with salt or strong jets of water—are available downstairs while tamer versions (reflexology, seaweed, and mud wraps) can be had upstairs. At $35/half hour, $60/hour, their Swedish massages are basic, but a great value.

You can easily lounge the day away here for the entrance fee of $22, alternating cool showers or a chilly dip with various degrees of heat. I emerged long after dark with cleansed pores and a sweet sense of exhaustion. Devotees can buy 15 admissions for $165, but watch out, as there are two owners who alternate taking charge from week to week, and you may find that a pass you bought last week while owner A was in charge will not be honored by owner B. A three-month membership is $260 and the whole place can be rented after hours for parties (10pm-4am) at $50 a head with a 20-person minimum. Call Lev Solon, 718-946-7618, for more information on group rentals. —*SCCC*

268 East 10th Street between 1st Avenue and Avenue A
212-674-9250
M-F: 11am-10pm; Sa-Su: 7am-10pm
(Men only: Su: 7:30am-2pm; women only: W: 8am-2pm
$22 admission fee)
www.russianturkishbaths.com

for a while, but, for us, lying down, more effectively promotes the flow of sexual energy.

On the way home in a cab at some ungodly hour, we reflected on the evening. The concept was great, the guests were sexy, and the ambiance very erotic, but we could have done without all the cigarette smoke, and, as noted, would have liked more space to lie down and play. Also, we noticed that not everybody played by the rules (at least one couple did not exit together, which is a no-no) and at least one man arrived unaccompanied by a woman. We have faith, though, that One Leg Up will continue to perfect its formula and we look forward to a return visit. —*SAL/TH*

Wall Street Sauna

1 Maiden Lane, 11th floor, west of Broadway
212-233-8900
M-F: 11am-8pm; Sa: noon-6pm; closed Su
Room rental (4 hours): $17; changing room (4 hours): $14;
locker: $11; 5-day locker pass: $40; if you're a
member of the East Side Club (see pg. 199), call for
a schedule of discounted rates

DESPITE ITS LOCATION JUST TWO BLOCKS FROM the site of the former World Trade Center, the management of Wall Street Sauna says business has tapered off only slightly in the wake of the September 11th terrorist attacks.

Like the East Side Club, this place is a bathhouse—a place where men go to have sex with men. A good portion of the clientele is middle aged or older, with most in their 50s, but you can find quite a few hunky younger men who typically offer a "straight" persona to the outside world. Here they can indulge in their fantasies or at least watch others indulging in theirs.

The Wall Street Sauna's facilities occupy two floors, and consist of rooms, common areas, and locker areas.

The rooms are actually cubicles with 8-foot-high partial walls furnished, with a bed. The changing rooms are slightly smaller with benches instead of beds.

The dress code is a towel—only a towel—which is issued when you pay at the front desk. Patrons can relax in one of the common areas—one of which features a monitor showing porn flicks—or they can cruise the halls, checking out the other patrons. Body language rules in bathhouses—there are no words, just eye contact and suggestive motions. If it's your room, invite someone in who strikes your fancy. If it's his room, wait until you're invited. And a final note on etiquette: no cruising in the toilet areas.

The Wall Street Sauna has one small sauna and one shower stall. The floors are a bit dirty, so bring sandals. —*MJN*

The West Side Club

27 West 20th Street between 5th and 6th Avenues
212-691-2700
24 hours a day, 7 days a week
Annual membership card (required for admission): $30;
day pass: $10; room rental (4 hours): $16; changing room
(4 hours): $14; locker charge: $11 (note that prices are
$2 higher from 2pm Friday until Sunday at midnight)

CONSIDERED THE PREMIER GAY BATHHOUSE IN New York City because of its Chelsea location, the West Side Club sports a diverse crowd weighted towards the young and stacked. Sometimes these humpy boys only want to have sex with each other, but often they're looking for something other than a mirror image of themselves. There are plenty of average guys, too—of all ages, ethnicities, and body types. In short, nobody but the unspeakably repulsive should have any trouble finding action here.

If you don't have a membership, bring a photo ID. During peak hours (late nights and weekends), you may

Donnie Russo

"**D**ADDY OF DADDIES" DONNIE RUSSO BRISTLES somewhat at the suggestion that for most of two decades his specialties have been fetish films and images. But, undeniably, Russo got his start in the early '80s doing nude modeling and posing for spreads for publications like Inches and Honcho. He launched a career in porn films in 1990 then the subsequent Internet explosion earned him more money and gave him more exposure than he ever imagined. On the New York scene, Russo has scaled back personal appearances in local nightclubs and benefits, but he certainly doesn't shy away from public exposure. "People know where I live, they see me around the neighborhood, and walking around the Village", he says. "I don't hide."

Gazing at recent photographs of his well-muscled physique, one can't help but notice his biblical tattoos, including an enormous and detailed Christ image on his back and rosary beads around his neck. "I consider myself spiritually strong," says Russo, "but I don't believe in organized religion." Russo keeps his personal life private, saying only that he's been "partnered for years." After decades of allowing his fans to drool over every inch of his beautiful body, Donnie Russo, pre-eminent leather daddy, is entitled to some degree of privacy. —MJN

You can view Donnie at his website: www.donnierusso.com

have to wait in line to check in at the window, where you pay your admission and leave your valuables in a locked drawer (be sure to tip the cute counter boys upon checking in and checking out—it's the gentlemanly thing to do). You are then given a towel (with condoms and lube on request) and shown to your room, changing room, or locker. Some guys choose to wander the two-floor labyrinth of corridors in their undershorts, but towels are the standard attire.

The West Side Club can be a friendly place where sex does not have to be cold, detached, or anonymous, although some patrons like it that way. Many of the guys are regulars, greeting and chatting with old buddies in the corridors. The staff is friendly, helpful, attractive, and apparently 100% gay, which is a nice change from some public sex scenes where sleazy straight guys take your money and admit you through a turnstile with a blank stare.

The facilities are clean, with sauna and steam room recently reopened after a long hiatus (per the Board of Health, thank you very much). The music—hard-driving techno with a hip-hop edge—proves to be an equally effective complement to bone dancing as it is to the disco kind. There are a few pieces of workout equipment that nobody uses, and a common area for continuous viewing of porn videos. Some regulars consider the upstairs rooms most desirable because they're closer to the showers and are more heavily traveled. But, downstairs has its appeal with its more secluded ambiance—a hint of an illicit backroom in a place where most taboos don't exist.

You can have tons of great sex at the West Side Club, but on your way home you may also remember the enjoyable 20 minutes or 2 hours you may have spent cuddling and chatting with a cute boy from the city or visiting from thousands of miles away. They all come to the West Side Club, from every country on every continent, even (especially!) if they're only spending a few days in New York. It's a place to rub elbows—so to speak—with a rich and varied cross section of gay men from the city, the country, and the world. And as a way to have uninhibited sex with strangers, it's much safer than hooking up at a bar and going back to his place or yours. Just remember your safer sex guidelines and keep in mind that guys don't always tell the truth about things like HIV status when they know they'll never have to face you again. Be clear about your own standards and limits, stick to your guns, and have fun. —*MHB*

The Oldest Profession, Gotham Style

DESPITE THE CITY'S EFFORTS TO CURB "QUALITY-OF-life crime," the oldest profession continues to thrive in New York—it's just a little harder to find the practitioners these days. Now we're not here to debate whether prostitution is right or wrong, whether it demeans women, whether it's feminism in action, or whether it's no different from the way most of us sell ourselves between 9 and 5, Monday to Friday. What we will tell you, though, is that it's illegal. It's also risky. Getting caught can carry some stiff penalties, not to mention public embarrassment. The writers and publishers of this guide do not endorse the buying and selling of sex between consenting adults, and assume no responsibility for any actions you might undertake on your own.

That said, the scene breaks down into three general categories: streetwalkers, the classic "hookers" and "hustlers" who hang out on street corners and ask you for a date; escort services, where the girl (or guy) comes to you; and in-call services, where you go to them.

Patronizing streetwalkers is, in general, a very bad idea. Aside from the fact that it makes you an easy target for the vice squad, it also puts you in real physical danger. No one walks the streets unless out of necessity. Streetwalkers tend to be drug addicts (who are known to rip off their customers), runaways, impoverished single mothers, and other desperate types. And as far as looks go, they tend to be at the bottom of the heap. And streetwalkers tend not to be too particular about condom use, so you best be. Even if you're tempted by the low cost of the services provided, or by the thought of doing something this sleazy, think again.

Escort services, on the other hand, are discreet and relatively safe, but pricey. Although many services will send a second girl (or boy) if you don't like the first one that shows at your door, you usually have to pay for the cab fare of the reject. And it's not like you can call Consumer Affairs if the service keeps sending you ugly dates. There's also the additional cost of a hotel room, since, risky business aside, it's just not a good idea to invite an escort into your home. Finding an escort service is easy, though: Just look in the back of the *Village Voice*, *New York Press*, or another free weekly, or do a search on the Internet.

"In-call" is the current euphemism for a whorehouse. They're trickier to find than escort services, but believe us: there are dozens of nondescript apartments all over the city doubling as brothels. They are found either by word of mouth or through listings in sex rags carried by most adult video stores. At brothels, expect to be searched at the door—standard procedure to make sure you're neither a cop nor out to rob them. The upside of visiting these establishments, if there is one, is that you can select from a choice of partners, and prices are generally a bit lower than they would be for an escort.

A few words of caution: kissing on the mouth is often, though not always, verboten. It's considered too intimate an activity. Secondly, always be polite. Never do anything rough, or that you haven't discussed with your service provider beforehand. Above all, treat him or her with respect—selling a service, even an intimate one such as this, does not make a person bad or "dirty". Courtesy is also common sense: there's usually muscle of some sort nearby. Like it or not, using the services of a prostitute means you're making a foray into the criminal underworld.

Tipping is not required, but encouraged—usually 15 to 20 percent—unless you've chosen one of the high-priced escort services, in which case as much as a few hundred over the suggested amount isn't unreasonable. Besides being the polite thing to do, tipping will establish you as a serious customer and make the girl and the service more responsive to you in the future. As with most things in this world, money talks and bullshit walks; in this scene, that goes double.

For more resources and advice from experienced johns, we recommend the World Sex Guide (www.worldsexguide.org). And for a directory of escorts, point your browser to www.eros-ny.com or www.ny-exotics.com. —TT

Youth Erotica

212-591-1103
Admission: generally $80 per couple
www.youtherotica.com
youngswingersNYC@yahoogroups.com (list serve)
youtherotica@yahoo.com

♀♂

"YOUTH EROTICA" MAY CONJURE IMAGES OF NU-bile bodies frolicking in G-strings, but this club is actual-ly a locus of private-party activity for adult swingers held at rotating locations, including hotels and even bed and breakfasts.

Billing itself as "the hottest New York youth club" makes Youth Erotica sound like a high school dance in the YMCA rather than the intimate and quiet party we attended. The website, complete with online pictures of past orgies, emphasizes that members should be "in good shape, sexy, and cultured," and also stipulates that parties are for "couples and beautiful single women only." But don't let such "requirements" deter you from further exploration. Our experience was that whoever paid at the door, got in, no questions asked.

The hosts, Sagi (he's a Sagittarius) and Redcat, formed Youth Erotica in 2001, after the disbanding of Tantra, a long-running swing group that had been Redcat's brain-child. According to her, Youth Erotica, like Tantra, serves as both an ethereal and physical stimulant of touch, taste, smell, and perception. Wow.

On a chilly Saturday afternoon in January, we called the Youth Erotica hotline to find out the location of that evening's party. This reviewer and her partner slid into a well-appointed Upper West Side hotel at 10pm, doing our best, as instructed, to slip by the concierge. We found ourselves sharing the elevator with another couple who looked as displaced as we did. I noticed her sexy red boots while she complimented my strappy rhinestone-studded stilettos. It was no surprise when we exited on the same floor.

After making a visual assessment and comparing notes on who were the most attractive guests, we lounged in the suite with a dozen other couples, all still fully dressed, nibbling grapes and cheese, sipping wine (BYOB), and listening to Madonna croon "Erotica" in the background.

My partner thought I was overdressed in a bustier and floor-length chiffon skirt, but I thought it comparable to one woman's skin-tight, mini pleather dress and another's gold-sequined attire. Dressed up or casual, ranging in age from early 20s to 50s, some couples seemed to already know each other, while other firsttimers, like ourselves, kept to the corners waiting for something to happen.

And happen it did. A young buck suddenly jumped up from the couch, dragging his partner into the bedroom. Quite the voyeurs, we trailed in behind them, situating ourselves on the periphery to watch their awkward fumbling and groping. The couple we had shared the elevator with invited us to join them, caressing my arm to make their intentions known. Instead, I buried my face in my partner's chest and hoped they would go away.

Redcat then orchestrated a brief warm-up exercise, instructing everyone to climb onto the king-size bed, still clothed, close their eyes, and experience the sensation of touch with those around them. The room quickly warmed up, at first not from sexual intensity but from the sheer density of bodies per square foot. I found myself removing my shirt (and later, skirt) to find relief from the oppressive heat.

With the ice broken, the party rolled on, taking with it clothes and inhibitions. Then, in the midst of this horizontal tango, a hotel management raid dispersed most of

the partygoers to another location, leaving us and two other straggling couples behind. It seemed a few people forgot to sneak into the hotel as instructed and had approached the front desk, foolishly announcing their destination with a line such as "Excuse me, but we're here for the swing party in room 519."

Near midnight and with the party flagging like a limp member, Sagi and Redcat urged us to stay, confident that more couples would show up for round two, while subtly implying they'd like to get to know us better. Eventually two new couples did join the mix while another made a brief appearance before backpedaling out the door. The female member of the duo refused to enter the room, clutching her mittens in a death grip, clearly at a loss as to why her partner had dragged her to a swing party.

When we finally left, after a steamy session on an over-stuffed chair, the hosts invited us to their next party at a discounted price to make up for the premature withdrawal of guests earlier in the evening.

Swinging newbies beware! Youth Erotica is not for the faint of heart. Be prepared to participate and remember these essential rules: shower before you arrive; practice safe sex; couples must arrive, disrobe, and leave together; and respect the boundaries of others. If you and your partner are up for a sexual adventure and are curious about swinging, Youth Erotica will not disappoint. —SAL

ALPHABETICAL INDEX

NEW YORK

NEIGHBORHOOD INDEX